WHAT IS YOUR

HOW TO IMPROVE YOUR INTERACTIONS QUOTIENT

BY ZAVÉ DAVIS

LEGAL DISCLAIMER

WHAT IS YOUR IQ?

www.betterIQnow.com

Copyright © 2024 Zavé Davis & NeuEarth Media.

Paperback ISBN:

All rights reserved. No portion of this book may be reproduced mechanically, electronically, or by any other means, including photocopying, without permission of the publisher or author except in the case of brief quotations embodied in critical articles and reviews. It is illegal to copy this book, post it to a website, or distribute it by any other means without permission from the publisher or author.

References to internet websites (URLs) were accurate at the time of writing. Authors and publishers are not responsible for URLs that may have expired or changed since the manuscript was prepared.

Limits of Liability and Disclaimer of Warranty

The author and publisher shall not be liable for your misuse of the enclosed material. This book is strictly for informational and educational purposes only.

Warning – Disclaimer

The purpose of this book is to educate and entertain. The author and/or publisher do not guarantee that anyone following these techniques, suggestions, tips, ideas, or strategies will become successful. The author and/or publisher shall have neither liability nor responsibility to anyone with respect to any loss or damage caused, or alleged to be caused, directly or indirectly by the information contained in this book.

Medical Disclaimer

The medical or health information in this book is provided as an information resource only and is not to be used or relied on for any diagnostic or treatment purposes. This information is not intended to be patient education, does not create any patient-physician relationship, and should not be used as a substitute for professional diagnosis and treatment.

Publisher
10-10-10 Publishing
Markham, ON
Canada

Printed in Canada and the United States of America

DEDICATIONS

To my Mother, Mrs. Ann Guy Davis | Mother, Mentor, Friend, and Inspiration | (1925 – 2019)

Bonjour Madam,

I dedicate this book to you because I am the man that I am today. After all, you always taught me how to stay positive, work hard, be honest, and helpful, be a selfless human being, and Love God with All My Heart, Mind, Body, and Soul.

She Might Be Gone But Never Forgotten

You can shed tears that she is gone, Or you can smile because she has lived; You can close your eyes and pray that she will come back; Or you can open your eyes and see all that she has left; Your heart can be empty because you can't see her; Or you can be full of the love that you shared; You can turn your back on tomorrow and live yesterday; Or you can be happy for tomorrow because of yesterday; You can remember her and only that she is gone, Or you can cherish her memory and let it live on; You can cry, close your mind, be empty, and turn your back; Or you can do what she would want: smile, open your eyes, love, and go on.

David Harkins

ACKNOWLEDGMENTS

There is a new trend among authors to thank every famous person for inspiration, non-existent assistance, and/or some casual reference to the author's work. Authors do this to pump themselves up. So, on the off chance that this is helpful, I wish to thank the following people for promoting upward mobility, inspiring humanity to do better, and giving us the world that we have today:

- 2023 - The Cleveland Clinic, Strategies on a better Mental Health.
- 2024 – Positive Psychology, Thirteen EQ Exercises and Activities.
- 1992 – Alex Hailey, The Autobiography of Malcolm X.
- 1975 - The Holy Bible, The Book of Proverbs (King Solomon).
- 2024 - Marina Crouse Writes, 29 Memoir Writing Exercises and Prompts.

There are many more people I could thank, but time, space, and modesty compel me to stop here.

TESTIMONIALS

Zavé gave me really great direction and feedback on my project and built up my confidence to continue with my project with a belief it could be produced in the near future.

— Jennifer Lewis Atlanta, GA

How do you spell facilitator? Z-A-V-E; He wants his writers creative and free. He sets up the classes and waits for the masses of teaching and feedback. There's never a lack. He listens and hears all our worries and fears quick with a smile, maybe even a laugh. He tells you your "final" is now just a "draft," but you take it to heart. His advice is smart; he might digress with art or jazz, perhaps even sports or what drink he had. Guidance and collaboration lead us to the dance of celebration, creating a safe place for our inner selves to embrace John Legend impressions, trips around the globe, things like therapy and ghosts aren't left unprobed, nudists, cottage cheese, and rhinos, I mean, even an epic about dog embryos anyone or anything is up for grabs in our minds.

TESTIMONIALS

Zavé takes it in stride. He never maligns fiction of science, memoirs, and poems; he doesn't settle for stuff that's ho-hum. He's a writer too and shares his world view. He shares his dinos and thoughts on his mother; he's become like our brother. Outside of the class, we get a hall pass Omelettes on decks.

We discuss many subjects from Chewbacca the dog to Matthew's epilogue, boxing music, and maybe politics; a harmonica concert is just the fix we're glad. You got vaccinated; for the class, you created thank you, merci, gracias, danke schoen (shun); you deserve a big vacation. So, even on Zoom, we wish you the best a life full of love, wonder, and zest!

— **Lorraine Voshell Asheville, NC**

As the Author of this powerful Portrait Memoir about his Mother: The Anna Guy Story, Zavé takes the reader on a young talented woman's journey and how she navigates the dilemmas and trials to pursue her talents and creative muse. The Harlem Jazz Renaissance is the backdrop to Anna's curtain calls, which include a host of characters like Duke Ellington, Count Basie, the one and only Billie Holiday, and others.

Zavé: you've created a compelling page-turner that one cannot put down and a Masterpiece of which your mother would surely be proud!

— **Barbara McKinney Lawrenceville, GA**

ABOUT THE AUTHOR

ZAVÉ DAVIS

Awarded the Excellence in the Songwriters Workshop Award by the American Society of Composers, Authors, and Publishers (ASCAP), Songwriter-Producer of the all-important MLK Dream Song released on MLK Day in 2023, current Brand Owner of The Cuddlesaur Brand™, Author of The Cuddlesaur Adventures Children's Book Series in both 2D and 3D, Creator of the Brand's Cuddlesaur Animation Series (based on the Book Series) and Proud Author of his Mother's very powerful memoir: Anna And The Cool—Chronicling the Harrowing True Story of Ann Guy Davis and her pursuits for Fame and Fortune in Entertainment during the Jazz Renaissance Period in Harlem, New York at the height of World War II to the Civil Rights Struggle of Nineteen Forties and Fifties America.

As a former IT Consultant and current Serial Entrepreneur, Zavé founded his own IT Consulting Practice servicing the needs of both medium and large-scale Multinational Technology Companies, leading the QA Testing Effort in his latter years as Lead QA Engineer and Georgia Institute of Technology PMI Certified Project Manager.

ABOUT THE AUTHOR

Zavé has worked across multiple verticals and acted as client-facing liaison between the client and company for multiple projects simultaneously, and that is strategic test planning for Tech Companies in the Entertainment Industry. He has worked with SMEs and Multinationals with emphasis on mentoring, team building, and stakeholder partnering.

With the support of the Prestigious Callanwolde Fine Arts Center, a foundation located in Atlanta, Georgia, for which he has served for the past five years as a Writing Instructor for both the Creative Writing and Memoirs Writing Classes, this Award-Winning Author currently lives in the US but travels across the nation conducting seminars and workshops to help others realize their dreams of becoming a published Author.

With this book, he has shared his insights, years of experience, and an in-depth look at one's own need to change the narrative and trajectory of one's own life experience in many different areas to realize their potential for growth.

Previously, Zavé operated a myriad of ventures within the Entertainment and Tech space through his portfolio of online platforms NeuEarth Media | The Cuddlesaur Brand™ | The Cuddlesaur Brand on YouTube and on Amazon Prime Video Direct where he's not only been awarded Best New Project in 2022 but enjoys a viewership of thousands of Streaming Hours per month in the UK, Germany, and Japan.

As an Author, Brand Owner, Songwriter, Writing Instructor, and Chess Coach, Zavé is redefining what it means in life to be "Purposeful and Intentional" with his many interests and of service to his community, making a lasting impact on the greater communities and society at large.

TABLE OF CONTENTS

FOREWORD xv

1. UNDERSTANDING YOUR COMMUNICATION HISTORY 1

- A Journey of Reflection and Redemption Rewriting Your Difficult Interactions 1
- Getting an honest IQ Assessment from trusted source(s) 3
- Researching Self-Help Guides and Resources for Additional Support 7
- Navigating Anger and Hurt 8

2. ASSESSING YOUR EQ 11

- Journaling Your Emotional Intelligence (EQ) 11
- Rewriting your Emotional Intelligence or EQ Reactions 14
- Getting an Honest EQ Assessment from Trusted Resource(s) 16
- Research EQ Hierarchy and Apply Principles 18
- Observe Your Reactions & Record Your EQ Progress 20

3. YOUR EQ-IQ LINK 23

- Researching Your EQ-IQ Relationship 23

Table of Contents

- Journaling Revisited Feelings On Past Interactions 26
- Developing Your EQ-IQ Strategy 28
- Making a Conscious Effort to Implement New Strategy 31
- Giving Yourself Time to Breathe/Break Old Habits 34

4. THE EQ-IQ BOOST 37

- Journaling Interactions Strategy 37
- Assessing Your EQ Progress Post New Strategy 39
- Assessing Your IQ Progress Post New Strategy 42
- Combining the Two Efforts into One Strategy 45
- Your New United Front Post Assessment/Implementation 48

5. "3-Ps" TO BETTER INTERACTIONS 51

- The "3-Ps" (Practice, Practice, Practice) 51
- Journaling Your More Recent Interactions 54
- Assessing Recent Interactions Within Your New Comfort Zone ... 56
- Striking Up Conversations With Strangers (w/Safety) 58
- Journaling Your Conversations With Strangers 60

6. AVOIDING TRIGGERS 62

- Revisiting Uncomfortable Conversations 62
- Journaling Uncomfortable Conversations 64
- Replaying Scenarios for A Better Outcome 67
- Assessing Your Triggers 70
- Rinse & Repeat for Better Outcomes 73

7. CELEBRATE BETTER RESULTS! 76

- Reading & Celebrating Your Journal Progress 76
- Assessing Your EQ-IQ Improvements 79

Table of Contents

- Celebrating Yourself for Each Win! 81
- Giving Yourself More Time to Improve 83
- Journaling Milestones 85

8. SECURING YOUR DREAM JOB! 87
   - Mastering Emotional Intelligence 87
   - Doing Your Research/Reaching Out to Your Network 89
   - Setting Up The Interview for Your Dream Job 92
   - Applying You're New IQ & Measuring Success 94
   - Journaling Milestones of this Newfound Experience 96

9. ATTITUDE OF GRATITUDE CONCEPTS 99
   - Deploying Gratitude & Empathy in Your Interactions 99
   - Your Interactions have been Off The Charts! 101
   - Cultivating Soft Skills In Your Communications 103
   - Giving Yourself A Little Grace… & Time 105
   - Journaling Milestones 107

10. EQ - IQ MASTERY 110
    - You've Arrived Here 110
    - Empathetic Resilience: Journey to EQ Mastery 110
    - Leveraging Your New IQ 112
    - Everyday Life Can Be Rewarding 113
    - Entering Into Interactions Bliss! 115
    - Journey to Interactions Bliss: Mastering EQ & Amplifying Encounters 117

xiii

FOREWORD

Dear Reader...

Are ready for that next chapter in your evolution? Are you ready to turn the page, take control of how you interact, and relate to others in your orbit and beyond? Do you wish to take control of and/or even change the narrative about how others perceive you (justified or unjustified)?

Well, I have written just the book to help you in this New Future YOU evolutionary process!

WHAT IS YOUR IQ? by Zavé Davis is intended to help you understand where you've been, where you're going, and where you are currently in your journey to achieving more success and happiness in your life by taking a deep dive into how you communicate with others and ways to improve your emotional intelligence (EQ), which will surely transform your interaction quotient: **THE NEW "IQ!"**

Perhaps you've been passed over for that new leadership position at the company for which you've dedicated your entire life and career and thought you were sure to be a "shew-in" since you knew the

FOREWORD

team intimately and it's you that leadership calls upon when assessing your colleagues on the team, but for some inexplicable reason, you were passed over... yet again!

This experience of being passed over has left you with a sense of betrayal and utter confusion, so now you're looking to move on from this company for which you've worked so hard to become a valued member in hopes that your efforts and contributions wouldn't go unrecognized.

Maybe there are situations, that have left you in a state of perplexity and you're in sheer wonderment about how some of your most valued relationships with family members and close friends have devolved into non-existence as a result of interactions that have gone horribly wrong OR you continue to doubt and/or question yourself after suffering the humiliation of a contentious divorce and are left wondering whether you will ever get back on that horse again since you have developed trust issues; if it included minor children, it was more painful than you could imagine.

This book will encourage you to challenge yourself and begin to develop strategies to become better at interacting with others, whether they be family, friends, or colleagues. It will serve as a guide in assessing your emotional intelligence (EQ) and give you clues into boosting and improving this often ignored aspect of one's psyche to promote a deeper understanding into a more meaningful interaction quotient (IQ). You will learn how journaling could help you in your quest for more meaningful relationships.

— **Raymond Aaron**
Leading Transformational Success Mentor
New York Times Best-Selling Author

CHAPTER 1

UNDERSTANDING YOUR COMMUNICATION HISTORY

A JOURNEY OF REFLECTION AND REDEMPTION
REWRITING YOUR DIFFICULT INTERACTIONS

In the depths of my self-reflection, I embark on a journey to revisit the tangled web of relationships that have defined my existence. Each thread is woven with love, pain, joy, and regret, forming the intricate tapestry of my life.

Family is the cornerstone of my being, yet also the source of profound anguish. Memories of heated arguments, bitter disagreements, and emotional distance haunt my thoughts. In those moments of anger and frustration, words were hurled like daggers, leaving wounds that time alone could not heal. How I long to turn back the hands of time, to rewrite those moments with empathy, kindness, and understanding.

Friends, once pillars of support, now just distant echoes of the past.

UNDERSTANDING YOUR COMMUNICATION HISTORY

Misunderstandings fueled by pride and ego-driven utterances placed wedges between our once solid bond, fracturing that which was once thought to be unbreakable. I see now the importance of humility, of swallowing my pride and extending that olive branch of mutual respect.

As I stand at the precipice of introspection, I realize the transformative power of empathy and vulnerability. To empathize is to step into the shoes of another, to see the world through their eyes, and feel their pain as my own. It is a humbling experience, one that opens the door to forgiveness, understanding, and reconciliation.

With vulnerability comes courage—the courage to lay bare my soul, to acknowledge my shortcomings, and to seek forgiveness with an open heart. No longer will I hide behind the walls of pride, ego, and defensiveness. Instead, I choose to embrace my imperfections and strive for authentic connections built upon a foundation of honesty, integrity, and compassion.

To my family and friends, I offer my sincerest apologies for the difficult part of our interactions to which I contributed. I may not be able to erase the past, but I can choose to create a future filled with love, acceptance, and reconciliation. Let us embark on this journey together, armed with empathy and vulnerability, as we rewrite the narrative of our relationships with grace and humility.

I'd like to begin this new dialogue with these thoughts in mind so that we can enjoy a future where we return to more trusting and meaningful interactions, once enjoyed prior to when our communication devolved into what it is now. You have my commitment and full participation from today on to rewrite that narrative of our interactions so that we can return to those happier moments. I know all of you impacted by this estrangement arrangement left by years of pain and trauma will agree with me when I say that we're missing out on the best part of our lives since we've experienced exponential growth since the last time we've chatted until now. We have so much to catch up on, so let's start planning that "catch-up moment," which could begin with coffee or tea!

GETTING AN HONEST IQ ASSESSMENT FROM TRUSTED SOURCE(S)

After you've revisited memories of some of your most painful and difficult interactions from the previous section, there are two surefire methods to begin work on improving your IQ, which could render measurable results in the short term.

Method 1:
A Heart-To-Heart Conversation with A Trusted Confidant.

Let me give you a somewhat familiar scenario that I feel we've all experienced in our interactions at one time or another in our lives. Although the names have been changed to protect the privacy of the actual individuals involved in the interactions, it might go like this:

Imagine a cozy living room with two comfortable armchairs facing each other and a briskly lit fireplace with fresh-cut wood on the fire. Soft lighting from a nearby lamp casts a warm glow.

Sitting on one chair, we'll call her SARAH, a woman in her late 30s, looking thoughtful yet apprehensive. Across from her sits her best friend and longtime trusted confidant, EMILY, with a compassionate expression, knowing they've relied on each other for similar discussions in the past.

UNDERSTANDING YOUR COMMUNICATION HISTORY

Sarah: [Sighs, fidgeting nervously] Emily, I need to talk to you about something… It's been weighing on my mind for a while now.

Emily: [Reaches out, placing a comforting hand on Sarah's knee] Of course, Sarah. You know you can talk to me about anything. What's on your mind? A new boyfriend? Issues with work?

Sarah: [Looks down, gathering her thoughts] Well, I've been reflecting on some of my past interactions with people, and I can't help but feel like I've missed the mark sometimes. I've had difficult conversations that didn't go as planned, and it's left me feeling unsure of myself.

Emily: [Nods understandingly] It's brave of you to acknowledge that, Sarah. We all have moments where we wish we could have handled things differently. Can you give me an example?

Sarah: [Pauses, choosing her words carefully] There was this incident at work where I had to give feedback to a colleague, and it turned into a heated argument. Looking back, I realize I might have come across as too confrontational, and it escalated unnecessarily.

Emily: [Listens attentively, nodding in empathy] I see. It's tough when emotions run high, especially in professional settings. But recognizing where things went off course is a transformational step towards growth and progress for a better Interactions Quotient (IQ).

Sarah: [Exhales, feeling relieved] Yeah, as always… you're right. I guess I just needed some perspective on it. It's been eating away at me, and I don't want to repeat the same mistakes.

Emily: [Offers a reassuring smile] You're not alone in this, Sarah. We've all been there. And you know what? You're doing the best you can with the tools you have. But if you're open to it, I'd be happy to offer some constructive criticism and help you navigate future interactions more effectively.

Sarah: [Gratefully] I'd really appreciate that, Emily. Your insight means a lot to me as you know.

Emily: [Encouragingly] Alright, let's start by exploring some communication techniques and strategies together. And remember, it's okay to stumble along the way. What matters is that you're committed to learning and growing from each experience.

[They continue their conversation, delving into specific scenarios and discussing actionable steps for improvement. As they talk, Sarah's confidence begins to strengthen, knowing she has a supportive friend by her side.]

Method 2: Write a letter or email sharing your thoughts on your past interactions and attach it to anyone whom you feel would accept your heartfelt humility and respond in kind.

It would look a little something like the following:

Header:

Seeking Constructive Feedback for Better Interactions

Introduction:

Dear Friends, Family, and Confidants,

I hope this message finds you well. As I reflect on past interactions and conversations, I recognize that there have been times when the exchanges might have been difficult or even painful for those

UNDERSTANDING YOUR COMMUNICATION HISTORY

involved. In my journey of personal growth and self-improvement, I am reaching out to you, my trusted circle, to provide honest and constructive feedback.

Background:

I acknowledge that communication is a complex art, and despite my best intentions, there may have been instances where my words or actions have caused discomfort or misunderstanding. Whether it was a heated debate, a sensitive topic, or simply a misunderstanding, I value your perspectives on how I can navigate future interactions with more empathy, clarity, and respect.

Request for Feedback:

I invite you to share your thoughts, observations, and suggestions regarding our past interactions. Your feedback is invaluable to me, as it will guide me in becoming a better communicator and a more compassionate individual. Specifically, I would appreciate insights on:

- How my words or actions impacted you during difficult conversations.
- Areas where I could have communicated more effectively or sensitively.
- Any recurring patterns or behaviors that you have noticed.
- Suggestions for improvement or strategies for better interaction in the future.

Assurance:

Please know that your feedback will be received with an open heart and without judgment. I am committed to growth and positive change, and I deeply value the input of those who know me best.

UNDERSTANDING YOUR COMMUNICATION HISTORY

Your honesty and candidness will contribute to a stronger, more harmonious relationship moving forward.

Closing:

Thank you for taking the time to participate in this process of self-reflection and improvement with me. Your support and guidance mean the world to me, and I am eager to learn from your experiences and perspectives. Together, we can foster healthier and more meaningful connections.

With gratitude and sincerity,

Your Name

RESEARCHING SELF-HELP GUIDES AND RESOURCES FOR ADDITIONAL SUPPORT

With any serious efforts to improve any aspect of your life, whether it be for personal or professional improvement, there comes the research phase. This is also true as it relates to the journey of bolstering your Interactions Quotient or IQ:

On the weekends, as some are out shopping or basking in the sun at a park, I like perusing the self-help section of a Borders Bookstore or a Barnes & Noble. This means finding something from that section to read while sipping my favorite latte or macchiato from a coffee store or bar.

There are plenty of references to becoming a better communicator or boosting your EQ or Emotional Intelligence for better Interactions or IQ, but I've yet to find a resource that puts all the pieces together, which is why I wrote this book in the first place.

So, I would begin my search in this section with titles that resonate with me at that moment to help me better understand the "why" and develop strategies.

NAVIGATING ANGER AND HURT: A JOURNEY TOWARDS UNDERSTANDING AND HEALING THROUGH SELF-HELP GUIDES

In moments of anger and hurt, interactions with individuals who trigger us can lead to painful conversations, leaving us feeling emotionally drained and disconnected.

However, seeking understanding and wisdom through self-help guides, both in bookstores and online, can be a transformative journey toward better interpersonal interactions and emotional well-being.

Anger is a complex emotion often triggered by perceived threats, injustices, or unmet needs. Identifying our triggers is the first step toward understanding our anger responses. Self-help guides offer valuable insights into recognizing and managing triggers, helping us gain clarity on the underlying causes of our emotional reactions.

Self-help resources encourage introspection and self-awareness, empowering us to recognize patterns of behavior and thought that contribute to our anger.

Techniques for emotional regulation, such as mindfulness and cognitive restructuring, are often explored in depth, providing practical strategies for managing intense emotions in the heat of the moment.

Developing empathy and compassion towards those who trigger us is essential for healthier interactions. Self-help guides often emphasize the importance of perspective-taking and understanding the motivations behind others' actions.

By cultivating empathy, we can foster deeper connections and navigate conflicts with greater understanding and grace. Effective communication is key to resolving conflicts and repairing relationships.

Self-help resources offer valuable guidance on assertive communication, active listening, and conflict resolution techniques. Learning to express our needs and boundaries assertively while respecting those of others can transform contentious conversations into opportunities for growth and reconciliation.

Healing from past hurts and forgiving both ourselves and others is a crucial aspect of personal growth toward a better IQ. Self-help guides provide tools for practicing self-compassion, forgiveness, and letting go of hardened resentment.

By releasing the grip of anger and embracing forgiveness, we free ourselves from the burden of emotional pain and open the door to deeper healing and emotional freedom.

In conclusion, embarking on a journey of self-discovery and growth through self-help guides can empower us to navigate anger-triggering interactions with greater wisdom and compassion. By cultivating self-awareness, empathy, and effective communication skills, we can transform hurtful conversations into opportunities for healing, understanding, and deeper connection with ourselves and others.

Once we gain momentum in this effort of cultivating our self-awareness, we become less and less prone to the triggers of the past, and this may actually lead us to feel better both emotionally and physically as stress is a byproduct of any unresolved resentment.

UNDERSTANDING YOUR COMMUNICATION HISTORY

This is where we should consider picking a trusted partner for practice at getting a better more amicable interaction and rehearse how to respond to certain triggers of the past that led to moments of anger, discomfort, and resentment.

CHAPTER 2

ASSESSING YOUR EQ

JOURNALING YOUR EMOTIONAL INTELLIGENCE (EQ)

In chapter 2 of *What Is Your IQ*, it's my belief that it's essential for one to assess their emotional intelligence since it's directly linked to a better overall intelligence and interaction quotient (IQ).

This work in assessing your emotional intelligence begins with journaling what you have experienced in the past within the context of your interactions with others, whether they be family, friends, colleagues, or just someone that you've met for the first time at the grocery store.

Just as you began revisiting those painful moments and memories where your interactions did not go well and sometimes resulted in gross misunderstandings or worse, I recommend that you use those same painful interactions and parse out if you can remember exactly what was said to begin the work of assessing the emotional intelligence component of the conversation.

ASSESSING YOUR EQ

If you're like me, where you find that your memories are both a blessing and a curse, then it would not be too difficult, especially where it concerns the more hurtful interactions, which led to months and often times years of resentment.

There are handy resources in the way of charts, graphs, and even pyramids, which I've found very useful in my journey, and now I would like to impart to you the same resources so that you can find yourself among the different levels of emotional intelligence.

Let me share one such resource with you below:

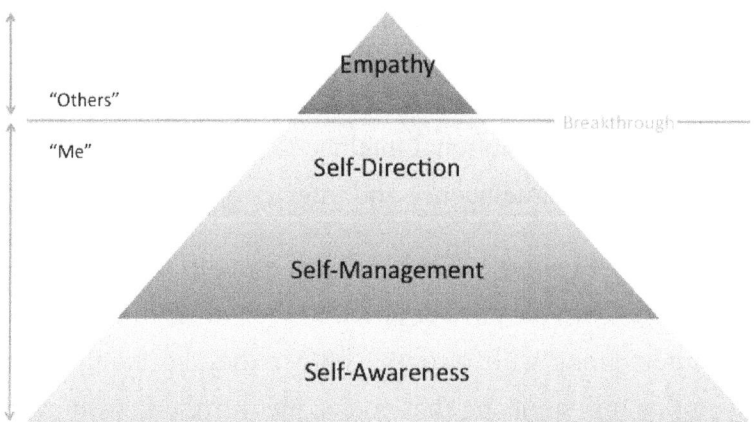

HIGH-LEVEL EQ PYRAMID

While most of us fall at the bottom of this EQ Pyramid, we could quickly improve our EQ, just as we could with our overall interaction quotient by doing crucial exercises to bolster our EQ.

As you can see, by this high-level EQ pyramid, self-awareness is something that is a given; however, most of us can remember a time when we took our self-awareness for granted and quickly went into a more reactive mode once the trigger points presented themselves in some of our most difficult interactions.

Do you often times walk away with the feeling of either not being heard or regretting something that was said, in anger or disappointment, as a result of perceived disrespect? Sometimes, difficult conversations are unavoidable, but as we approach doing the work it takes to avoid those triggers, we will quickly learn as we look back on it that our responses were the result of a reactive self-awareness posture. If you are anything like me, you value the impression you leave on others.

It is imperative for us to dig deep, make progress with our emotional intelligence, and approach this journey with utmost honesty and integrity about how UNself-aware we were during these times of painful interactions.

Later in this chapter, I will add another resource that shows our granular view of emotional intelligence so that you can get an idea of exactly where you fit and where you've been so that you can plot a course to where you are going.

But first, we will revisit those difficult times and interactions, which resulted in years of estranged relationships due to these painful interactions by rewriting or revisionist history, just as we did in chapter 1 on interactions. For our next section, this will be revisiting and rewriting our EQ.

REWRITING YOUR EMOTIONAL INTELLIGENCE OR EQ REACTIONS

Emotional intelligence (EQ) is crucial for navigating social interactions and fostering meaningful connections. It's the ability to recognize, understand, and manage our own emotions, as well as the emotions of others. Conversations can often be challenging, leading to misunderstandings and hurt feelings. Assessing your EQ in conversations can help you identify areas for improvement and cultivate healthier communication habits.

Self-awareness

Reflect on past conversations where emotions escalated, or hurt feelings ensued. Ask yourself:

- How did I contribute to the escalation of emotions?
- What emotions did I experience during the conversation?
- Did I accurately perceive the emotions of the other person?
- Were there any triggers that led to my emotional response?

Self-regulation

Evaluate your ability to manage your emotions during conversations:

- Did I remain calm and composed, or did I react impulsively?
- How effectively did I control my emotional reactions?
- Did I practice proactive listening and empathy towards the other person?
- Could I have handled the situation differently to prevent hurt feelings?

Empathy

Consider your capacity to understand and empathize with the emotions of others:

- Did I validate the other person's feelings, even if I disagreed with them?
- How well did I demonstrate empathy and understanding?
- Did I consider the impact of my words on the other person's emotions?
- Could I have shown more compassion towards their perspective?

Social Skills

Assess your ability to communicate effectively and build a rapport:

- Did I communicate my thoughts and feelings clearly?
- How well did I adapt my communication style to the other person?
- Did I prioritize collaboration and finding common ground in my conversation?
- Were there opportunities to de-escalate and work towards mutual understanding?

Action Plan

Based on your assessment, create a plan to improve your EQ in conversations:

- Practice mindfulness to enhance self-awareness and self-regulation.
- Develop active listening skills to better understand others' perspectives.

- Seek feedback from trusted friends or mentors to identify blind spots.
- Utilize techniques such as deep breathing or taking a pause to manage emotions during difficult conversations.
- Commit to laying a foundation for fostering a supportive and empathetic communication environment.
- Remember, improving your EQ is a journey that requires patience and practice.

By honing your emotional intelligence, you can cultivate healthier and more fulfilling relationships, both personally, professionally, and with complete strangers.

GETTING AN HONEST EQ ASSESSMENT FROM TRUSTED RESOURCE(S)

I find myself at a crossroads, grappling with the aftermath of several deeply painful interactions that have left scars on both my psyche and some of my most valued relationships. These encounters have tested not only my resilience but also my emotional intelligence—a facet of myself I now earnestly seek to understand and improve upon.

In recent times, I've found myself embroiled in situations fraught with tension and conflict. Emotions ran high, and in the heat of the moment, words were exchanged that cut deep. The aftermath revealed fractured relationships, hurt feelings, and a lingering sense of regret. I recognize that my own emotional responses played a significant role in escalating these situations to their painful conclusions.

In the aftermath of these encounters, I've taken a step back to reflect on my own emotional responses and behaviors. I've come to realize that while I may have valid emotions and concerns, how I express them can greatly impact the outcome of any interaction. In moments of intense emotion, I've often struggled to maintain composure and respond with empathy and understanding.

An honest assessment of my emotional intelligence reveals areas in need of growth and improvement. I recognize the importance of self-awareness—the ability to recognize and understand my own emotions in the moment. Equally crucial is self-regulation—the capacity to manage and control those emotions, especially in tense or challenging situations.

Furthermore, empathy—the ability to understand and share the feelings of others—is a cornerstone of healthy interpersonal relationships, one that I aspire to cultivate more deeply.

Armed with this newfound awareness, I am committed to actively developing my emotional intelligence. This journey will require patience, introspection, and a willingness to confront discomfort head-on. I understand that growth is often accompanied by discomfort, but I am determined to re-emerge from this process as a more emotionally intelligent individual.

These painful interactions I've experienced have served as a wake-up call, prompting me to delve deeper into the realm of emotional intelligence. While the road ahead may be challenging, I am steadfast in my resolve to cultivate greater self-awareness, self-regulation, and empathy. By doing so, I hope to not only mend fractured relationships but also foster healthier, more meaningful connections with those around me.

After you've journaled your "note to self," the first thing I would do is revisit that Sarah/Emily Conversation in Chapter 1, focusing your energy on boosting the EQ by responding to triggers quite differently than you did in the past, practicing not to be reactive. Record and listen.

RESEARCH EQ HIERARCHY AND APPLY PRINCIPLES: EXPLORING THE EQ HIERARCHY

Unraveling the EQ Hierarchy: A Journey of Self-Discovery

In an ever-evolving world, where success isn't merely defined by intelligence quotient (IQ) but by emotional intelligence (EQ) as well, delving into the EQ Hierarchy becomes paramount. This narrative chronicles a personal journey of exploration as one individual seeks to understand and apply the principles of EQ in their life.

The journey begins with understanding the foundational elements of emotional intelligence. Research into the core components—self-awareness, self-regulation, social awareness, and relationship management—provides a roadmap for personal growth. Through introspection and observation, the individual in pursuit of a higher EQ identifies areas for improvement and sets her intentions to cultivate these fundamental skills.

Monitoring Self-Discovery

Peeling back the layers of self-awareness unveils a deeper understanding of personal strengths and weaknesses. Embracing vulnerability, the individual confronts past traumas and limiting beliefs, paving the way for emotional healing and resilience. With newfound clarity, they embark on a transformative journey towards self-acceptance and authenticity.

Empathy and Compassion

As social awareness expands, empathy emerges as a guiding principle in interpersonal relationships. Through proactive listening and perspective-taking, the individual cultivates deeper connections with others, fostering empathy and compassion in both personal and professional interactions. Recognizing the interconnectedness of humanity, they strive to make a positive impact on the world around them.

Navigating Relationships

Relationship management becomes the focal point as the individual applies EQ principles to navigate complex social dynamics. From conflict resolution to effective communication, they employ empathy and emotional regulation to foster healthy, fulfilling relationships. By fostering trust and understanding, they cultivate a supportive network of peers, mentors, and allies.

The journey through the EQ Hierarchy is not merely a quest for personal development but a transformative odyssey of self-discovery and growth. Armed with a newfound understanding of emotional intelligence, the individual emerges empowered to navigate life's challenges with grace and authenticity. As they continue to apply EQ principles in their daily interactions, they inspire others to embark on their own journey toward emotional mastery.

In a world where success is measured not only by intellect but also by emotional resilience and empathy, exploring the EQ Hierarchy becomes essential. Through introspection, empathy, and authentic connection, individuals can unlock their full potential and create meaningful change in their lives, with their families, and in their communities.

Signs of Emotional Intelligence (EQ):

1. You think about others' feelings. Do you ever sense negative emotions in yourself or in others and stop to think what might have caused this?
2. You control your thoughts…
3. You are always authentic, no matter the situation or venue…
4. You pause to present a more thoughtful response…
5. You are empathetic…
6. You apologize immediately once you've recognized you're negative response…
7. You forgive…
8. You offer up suggestions to help the interaction…

Author's Note: This narrative serves as a testament to the transformative power of emotional intelligence and the profound impact it can have on personal and interpersonal growth.

OBSERVE YOUR REACTIONS & RECORD YOUR EQ PROGRESS

Observing My Response(s): A Path to Higher EQ

In the silence of self-awareness, I embark on a journey to unravel the intricacies of my emotional landscape. Armed with curiosity and introspection, I navigate through the maze of my feelings, seeking enlightenment and mastery over my emotional reactions and responses.

This endeavor isn't merely about deciphering the present moment; it's a deliberate effort to measure my reactions against the tapestry of my past experiences, paving the way for a higher Emotional Intelligence (EQ).

The Present Moment

Every emotion that surges through me is a clue, a signal from my inner self. In moments of joy, sorrow, anger, or fear, I pause, allowing myself to fully experience the depths of these sensations. Rather than letting them overwhelm me, I become a keen observer, dissecting the triggers and underlying causes behind each emotional wave.

Reflections from the Past

The past serves as both a teacher and a mirror. I delve into memories, recalling instances where similar emotions had once held power over me. Asking myself: how did I react then? What were the consequences of those reactions? By revisiting these moments, I gleaned insights into my patterns of behavior, identifying areas where I had stumbled and there were even moments where I had triumphed.

Measuring Growth

Emotional intelligence isn't static; it's a dynamic process of growth and refinement. Armed with the knowledge gained from introspection and retrospection, I measure my current reactions against those of the past. Have I learned from previous mistakes? Am I better equipped to navigate through turbulent emotional waters? Each moment becomes an opportunity for growth, a chance to inch closer to that seemingly elusive mastery over my emotions.

Cultivating Empathy

A crucial aspect of emotional intelligence is the ability to empathize, not just with others but also with oneself. I extend compassion towards my own vulnerabilities, acknowledging that imperfection is inherent to the human experience. This empathy forms the foundation upon which I build my understanding of others, fostering deeper connections and nurturing harmonious relationships.

The Path Forward

Armed with these insights gleaned from self-reflection and introspection, I tread forward on my journey toward emotional intelligence. It's a path fraught with challenges and obstacles, yet every stumbling block is a stepping stone towards growth. With each passing day, I inch closer to the elusive goal of mastering my emotions and forging a deeper understanding of myself and the world around me.

In the crucible of self-awareness, I forge the tools necessary to navigate the complexities of human emotion. With each observation, reflection, and measured response, I inch closer to the pinnacle of emotional intelligence, where serenity and wisdom reign supreme.

This page encapsulates the essence of observing one's emotional reactions and leveraging past experiences to cultivate a higher EQ. It serves as a testament to the transformative power of self-awareness and introspection in the pursuit of emotional mastery.

Please find the more comprehensive EQ Measure in the next chapter.

CHAPTER 3

YOUR EQ-IQ LINK

RESEARCHING YOUR EQ-IQ RELATIONSHIP:
EXPLORING THE RELATIONSHIP BETWEEN EMOTIONAL INTELLIGENCE & INTERACTIONS

Emotional Unity
(Pure Consciousness, Fullfilment & Emptyness)

Transcendence
(Self-Reflection, Transcendental Knowledge)

Universality of Emotions, Self-Actualization
(Self-Perfection, Self-Accomplishment)

Social Skills, Expertise in Emotions
(Problem-Solving, Reasoning, Social-Management)

Social-Awareness, Empathy, Discrimination of Emotions
(Awareness, Monitoring, Social Recognition & Flexibility)

Self-Management
(Self-Regulation, Flexibility, Self-Control)

Self-Awareness
(Self-Perception, Awareness, Self-Observation)

Emotion Recognition, Perception-Expression of Emotions
(Memory, Perception, Recognition, Labelling Emotions)

Emotional Stimuli
(Emotional Sensory Encoding, Attention)

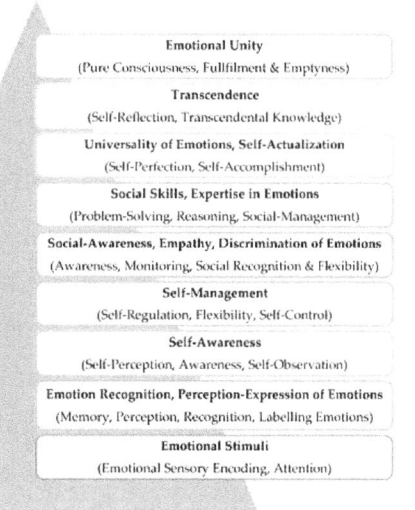

As many of you know, emotional intelligence is directly tied to interactions and outcomes. It can determine how you behave in conversations and what your responses are during those heated moments, rendering undesirable results in some of your most difficult interactions.

In this section, we will closely examine the relationship between some of your most contentious interactions and your responses that lead to their ultimate dire outcomes.

As we continue to parse out your responses to these contentious conversations, which have led to estrangement with some of your close personal relationships, we will engage in exercises that do the necessary analysis to understand where you are today, where you've been, and where you're going with this newfound effort to get your IQ where it needs to be towards a successful future.

In the intricate tapestry of human connections, I find myself tracing the threads of my own experiences, seeking to unravel the complex relationship between my Emotional Intelligence (EQ) and the tumultuous interactions that have, at times, led to the painful separation of friends and loved ones.

Emotional Intelligence, often described as the ability to recognize, understand, and manage our own emotions while effectively navigating the emotions of others, has emerged as a critical factor in fostering healthy relationships. Yet, despite my earnest endeavors, I have found myself ensnared in a cycle of misunderstandings and miscommunications, where the very qualities intended to foster connection often seem to drive a wedge between myself and those I hold dear.

Reflecting upon past encounters, I am struck by moments where my inability to effectively convey my emotions or to empathize with the feelings of others has resulted in fractures within relationships that once flourished.

Whether it was a failure to recognize the subtle nuances of nonverbal cues or an unchecked emotional response that led to unintended hurt, the consequences have been profound, leaving behind a trail of fractured bonds and lingering regrets.

As I embark on this journey of self-discovery, I am compelled to delve deeper into the intricate interplay between my EQ and the dynamics of interpersonal relationships. Through introspection and reflection, I aim to identify patterns of behavior and thought that may have inadvertently sabotaged these now-strained relationships.

Moreover, I recognize the importance of honing my emotional intelligence skills, not only for the betterment of my own well-being but also as a means of fostering more meaningful and fulfilling relationships with those around me.

By cultivating greater self-awareness, empathy, and emotional regulation, I aspire to forge connections rooted in understanding, compassion, and mutual respect.

Yet, I am mindful that this journey toward greater emotional intelligence is not one embarked upon in isolation. It is through open dialogue, sincere communication, and a willingness to embrace vulnerability that true growth and transformation can occur.

As I seek to mend the frayed threads of past relationships and weave new connections grounded in empathy and understanding, I am reminded that the pursuit of harmony within oneself and with others is a journey fraught with challenges but one imbued with the promise of profound personal growth and authentic human connection.

JOURNALING REVISITED FEELINGS ON PAST INTERACTIONS: A JOURNEY OF SELF-REFLECTION AND GROWTH

As in the previous chapters, we start by journaling our past difficult interactions and if we can remember those feelings associated with these contentious conversations.

What I like to focus on is after you have documented or journaled all that you could remember about some of your most difficult and contentious conversations with friends and loved ones, I want you to pay close attention to the feelings, revisiting these uncomfortable moments invoke.

Please remember to trust your feelings because feelings don't lie; they only allow you to experience what it felt like during the actual conversation. Someone said that the eyes are the windows to the soul. Well, in a similar fashion, your feelings are the emotions emanating from the soul.

Journal Entry:

In this journal, I embark on a deeply personal journey to confront past interaction trauma, seeking to understand the feelings associated with them and the lingering difficulties they have left in their wake. My aim is to not only revisit these painful experiences but also to use them as a catalyst for growth and self-improvement. By delving into these memories, I hope to gain insight into the mistakes I made and pave the way for a more fulfilling future.

As I delve into the depths of my memory, I confront moments where I felt hurt, misunderstood, or dismissed in interactions with others.

Each memory carries with it a wave of emotions—anger, sadness, regret, resentment…even shame. I allow myself to fully experience these feelings, acknowledging their impact on my psyche.

I reflect on how these past traumas have shaped my behavior and beliefs. I recognize patterns of self-doubt, fear of rejection, and a tendency to avoid certain situations, confrontations, or people.

These difficulties have often held me back from fully engaging with life and forming meaningful connections with others who've crossed my path.

With my newfound awareness, I commit to a course correction. I identify the mistakes I made in these past interactions; perhaps I failed to communicate effectively, set boundaries, or prioritize my own needs. Armed with this knowledge, I vow to approach my future interactions with greater mindfulness and intentionality.

Through this process, I come to see past traumas not as insurmountable obstacles but as opportunities for growth. Each interaction, no matter how painful, offers valuable lessons. I commit to embracing the lessons in these interactions with humility and grace, recognizing that they are essential stepping stones on my journey toward self-improvement.

As I close this section on my introspection, I feel a sense of liberation and empowerment!

By confronting my past interaction trauma head-on, I have taken a crucial step toward healing and personal growth. Armed with self-awareness and a renewed sense of purpose, I look forward to navigating future interactions with greater confidence and authenticity.

This journal serves as a testament to my resilience and determination to forge a brighter, more fulfilling future path forward for myself and hopefully spread this infectious self-love and introspection to those around me as well. It all begins in earnest in the next section of this book.

DEVELOPING YOUR EQ-IQ STRATEGY: ENHANCING INTERACTIONS THROUGH EMOTIONAL INTELLIGENCE

As with the previous chapters, there should always be a strategy for any and every serious effort that will bring about profound change and exponential growth in one's life.

In this section called Developing your EQ to IQ Strategy, we will explore ways in which we could bring about a better result by implementing our newfound wisdom after we've done the analysis of self-reflection on our prior emotional intelligence or EQ.

Not only will we come up with ways to combat those old habits, which have led to passing interaction trauma, but we will monitor each interaction for at least a few days to a week going forward once we decide to deploy this new strategy. Again, a partner in this effort is encouraged.

In today's dynamic world, success often hinges not only on technical skills but also on the ability to navigate social and emotional landscapes, something we refer to as soft skills.

Meet Jane, an ambitious professional seeking to elevate her interactions by harnessing the power of Emotional Intelligence (EQ) in the workplace.

Understanding that EQ plays a pivotal role in personal and

professional success, Jane is committed to developing a strategy that integrates EQ principles into her daily interactions.

As I fore stated, Emotional Intelligence (EQ) encompasses the ability to recognize, understand, and manage one's own emotions, as well as the capacity to perceive and influence the emotions of others.

Below is a real-world example of a high-level strategy implemented by Jane:

Jane recognizes that by honing her EQ skills, she can foster better communication, build stronger relationships, and achieve greater outcomes in both her personal and professional life.

Jane's strategy for deploying EQ concepts revolves around self-awareness, self-regulation, empathy, and social skills:

1. Self-Awareness: Jane begins by cultivating a deep understanding of her own emotions, strengths, and weaknesses. Through introspection and reflection, she identifies her triggers and patterns of behavior, enabling her to respond more effectively in challenging situations.

2. Self-Regulation: Armed with self-awareness, Jane practices self-regulation techniques to manage her emotions constructively. By staying composed under pressure and avoiding impulsive reactions, she maintains control over her interactions and decision-making processes.

3. Empathy: Jane actively seeks to understand the perspectives and emotions of others. By listening attentively, acknowledging feelings, and demonstrating empathy, she fosters trust and rapport in her interactions, leading to more meaningful connections.

4. Social Skills: Leveraging her enhanced emotional awareness and empathy, Jane hones her social skills to navigate various social contexts with finesse. She communicates assertively, resolves conflicts diplomatically, and collaborates effectively with diverse individuals, thereby maximizing synergy and productivity.

Jane's commitment to integrating EQ principles into her interactions yields tangible benefits:

1. Improved Communication: By understanding her own emotions and those of others, Jane communicates more effectively, fostering clarity and mutual understanding in her interactions.

2. Enhanced Relationships: Through empathetic listening and genuine connection, Jane builds stronger, more trusting relationships with colleagues, clients, and stakeholders, laying the foundation for collaboration and cooperation.

3. Conflict Resolution: Armed with heightened emotional awareness and social skills, Jane adeptly navigates conflicts and disagreements, transforming potential obstacles into opportunities for growth and consensus-building.

4. Increased Influence: By mastering the art of persuasion and negotiation, Jane exerts a positive influence on others, inspiring confidence and eliciting support for her ideas and initiatives.

In Jane's journaling of her journey to enhance her interactions through Emotional Intelligence, she discovers that EQ is not just a set of skills but a way of life. By embracing self-awareness, empathy, and social skills, she elevates her interactions to new heights, fostering a culture of collaboration, empathy, and mutual respect.

As Jane continues to refine her EQ strategy as she sees fit, she paves the way for personal growth, professional success, and meaningful connections in every facet of her life.

MAKING A CONSCIOUS EFFORT TO IMPLEMENT NEW STRATEGY: JOURNEY TO EMOTIONAL INTELLIGENCE (EQ) MASTERY

Jane's example in the previous section offers a reminder of the steps it takes to clearly and concisely implement your new strategy at a high level. What we will try to do in this section is to look at these steps in more granular detail with this same high-level strategy and cover ways to measure your progress at each step in the process.

What I'd like to do is caution the reader at this juncture in the process to not expect immediate results as you are embarking upon a journey to change behavior that's existed in your psyche for years and oftentimes decades even, so please proceed through this process with patience.

In our next example, we will see a more granular effort from someone we will call Emma:

Emma embarked on a transformative journey to enhance her Emotional Intelligence (EQ) for improved personal and professional interactions. Recognizing the significance of EQ in fostering meaningful relationships and achieving success, Emma implemented a deliberate strategy, fostering self-awareness, empathy, and effective communication.

1. Self-Assessment: Emma began by assessing her current EQ level through journaling, self-reflection, and feedback from trusted individuals. This involved identifying strengths and opportunities for improvement.

2. Educational Pursuits: She is committed to continuous learning through literature, online courses, and workshops focused on emotional intelligence, psychotherapy, and interpersonal skills. Emma gained insights into recognizing and managing emotions, understanding others' perspectives, and resolving conflicts constructively. She explores prayer and meditation as well.

3. Practical Application: Emma intentionally and proactively applied newfound knowledge in real-life scenarios. She practiced mindfulness techniques to regulate her emotions, actively listened to understand rather than respond, and engaged in empathy-building exercises to connect with others on a deeper level.

4. Feedback Loop: Emma sought feedback from peers, mentors, and colleagues to gauge her progress and refine her approach. Constructive criticism served as a catalyst for growth, enabling her to adapt and evolve her strategies continuously.

5. Cultivating Relationships: She prioritized nurturing meaningful connections by investing time and effort in understanding others' emotions and perspectives. Emma fostered a supportive environment where open communication and mutual respect thrive, leading to stronger personal and professional relationships.

6. Conflict Resolution Skills: Emma honed her ability to navigate conflicts effectively by employing techniques such as proactive

listening, reframing perspectives, and seeking win-win solutions. She embraced difficult conversations with empathy and assertiveness, fostering resolution and understanding.

7. Enhanced Interpersonal Relationships: Emma experienced deeper connections and trust in her personal and professional relationships, fostering collaboration and mutual respect.

8. Improved Communication: Her refined communication skills enabled Emma to convey thoughts and emotions effectively, leading to a clearer, more concise understanding and reducing the possibility of misunderstandings.

9. Conflict Resolution Success: Emma successfully navigated challenging situations with composure and empathy, transforming conflicts into opportunities for growth and understanding.

10. Professional Growth: Her heightened EQ positively influenced her soft skills, leadership style, decision-making, and teamwork abilities, contributing to career advancement and organizational success.

Notice the differences in Jane's and Emma's Strategies; pick and choose what works for you as you could always go back and tweak it for better results at a later date.

In conclusion, Emma's intentional pursuit of emotional intelligence (EQ) has resulted in profound personal and professional growth.

Through a strategic approach focused on self-awareness, empathy, and effective communication, Jane and Emma have transformed their interactions, fostering deeper connections, resolving conflicts constructively, and achieving greater success in all facets of their lives.

GIVING YOURSELF TIME TO BREATHE/BREAK OLD HABITS

Building New Bridges: A Journey to Empathetic Communication

In this last section of chapter 3, we will discuss the importance of giving yourself time to break the old habits that have accumulated over the years and gained momentum over times of learned, observed, and practiced behavior spanning throughout the bulk of our lives.

Whether we observed our parents engaging in heated arguments, which devolved into hurtful outcomes, or whether we ourselves engaged in discussions as a direct result of learned behavior, we all just need to Breeeeeeeeathe! The time for your change is NOW, and it begins TODAY!

Take a step back and channel a new energy to not be in your parent's marriage or your uncle's relationship. Take a minute to revisit those contentious meetings, which ultimately led to your firing or forcing you to resign over what you termed "office politics!" After all, it was difficult to let go since you came into this opportunity thinking you were on your way to experiencing your dream job and the success that comes along with all that, so this had a profound impact on you.

This section encapsulates the transformational journey of an individual who is committed to breaking free from old communication habits rooted in past traumas. Shaped by experiences of poor emotional intelligence (EQ) in childhood and early career stages, she now embarks on a quest for personal growth and healthier interactions.

Through introspection and mindfulness, she seeks to rewrite her narrative, fostering empathy, understanding, and positive outcomes in her relationships:

1. Trauma-Informed Communication: Recognizing the impact of past experiences on present communication patterns, she acknowledges the need to heal and evolve.

2. Emotional Intelligence (EQ) Development: Prioritizing and journaling self-awareness, self-regulation, empathy, and social skills, she embraces the journey of enhancing her EQ to navigate interactions more effectively.

3. Mindful Communication: Embracing the power of mindfulness, she learns to pause, breathe, and reflect before responding, fostering clarity and intentionality in her communication.

4. Changing the Narrative: By challenging old scripts and reframing perspectives, she aims to shift from reactive to proactive communication, empowering herself to create positive outcomes.

5. Building Empathetic Bridges: Cultivating empathy and understanding, she seeks to bridge gaps, strengthen connections, and foster healthier relationships in both personal and professional spheres. This requires a Mission Statement and a mention of the Key Takeaway:

Mission Statement:

"To break free from the chains of past communication patterns, I commit to embracing mindfulness, empathy, and emotional intelligence (EQ). With each interaction, I strive to breathe, reflect, and rewrite my narrative, fostering understanding, connection, and growth."

Key Takeaway:

Through conscious efforts and a commitment to personal growth, individuals can break free from old communication habits, transcend past traumas, and cultivate healthier, more empathetic interactions, thus shaping a brighter future for themselves and those around them.

CHAPTER 4

THE EQ-IQ BOOST

JOURNALING INTERACTIONS STRATEGY

So now that you've implemented this new EQ-IQ Strategy, you want to gauge your progress with certain interactions post-new strategy implementation.

How does one gauge progress? By carefully choosing those interactions with individuals with whom you haven't had a history of great communication; in fact, I would encourage you to seek out those in your family, among your friends, and/or colleagues that you would typically endure for the sake of keeping peace with individuals and reengage for the purpose of better dialogue.

If you feel that you're not yet ready to engage with these individuals, then I would say have a trusted friend, BFF, or confidant— someone whom you've chosen at the start of this journey who's familiar with your new effort to do a bit of role-play and assume the role of that individual with whom you've experienced triggers in your interactions.

Below is an example of implementing your new strategy and journaling your progress:

Objective:

To enhance interactions with family, friends, and colleagues by implementing strategies to improve Emotional Intelligence (EQ) and effectively manage challenging interactions.

Methodology:

1. Engage in regular self-reflection to identify emotional triggers and patterns of behavior in difficult interactions.
2. Practice proactive listening and perspective-taking exercises to better understand the emotions and viewpoints of others.
3. Employ techniques such as deep breathing, mindfulness, and cognitive reframing to manage intense emotions during conflicts.
4. Learn and apply assertive communication, conflict resolution, and boundary-setting techniques to navigate challenging interactions constructively.
5. Seek feedback from trusted individuals and integrate learnings from successes and setbacks into ongoing EQ development.

Results:

1. Improved Conflict Resolution: Successfully resolved conflicts with family members by approaching discussions with empathy and open-mindedness, leading to a deeper understanding and compromise.
2. Strengthened Relationships: Fostered closer bonds with friends through proactive listening and validation of their emotions, resulting in increased trust and support in relationships.

3. Enhanced Team Dynamics: Cultivated a more positive work environment by effectively managing disagreements and promoting collaboration among colleagues, leading to improved productivity and morale. Show off your newfound soft skills.
4. Personal Growth: Experienced greater emotional resilience and self-confidence in navigating difficult interactions, contributing to overall well-being and satisfaction in personal and professional situations.

The implementation of EQ improvement strategies has yielded tangible benefits in interpersonal relationships, fostering deeper connections and more constructive interactions with family, friends, and colleagues. Continued commitment to self-awareness, empathy, and effective communication will further enhance emotional intelligence and enrich both personal and professional experiences.

ASSESSING YOUR EQ PROGRESS POST NEW STRATEGY

Emotional Intelligence (EQ) Assessment and Reconciliation Plan

Just as you would with any monitoring of progress across all important areas of your life; whether that be personal or professional, it is imperative that you apply these same principles to your EQ progress by assessing how far you've come and plotting a course to how far you'd like to go.

Your EQ is no exception as you will see in the longterm this will translate far beyond your normal day-to-day interactions. I would go even further to say that any progress you make in any aspect of your life makes you feel good about yourself and begins to change the narrative about you.

Taking stock of your own mental and emotional health and well-being shows that you not only care about yourself but also the people in the surrounding environment with whom you interact.

Objective:

To evaluate the effectiveness of implemented EQ improvement strategies and initiate the healing process in past interactions by reengaging with individuals where previous interactions were challenging at best and oftentimes traumatic, leading to hurtful outcomes and resentment.

Assessment Process:

1. Self-Reflection: Review past interactions and identify specific instances where EQ skills were tested or lacked effectiveness.

2. Emotional Inventory: Assess personal emotional responses and triggers during past interactions, noting areas for improvement.

3. Impact Analysis: Reflect on the impact of past interactions on relationships and personal well-being, acknowledging any lingering emotional distress or trauma.

4. Skill Evaluation: Evaluate the application of EQ strategies in recent interactions and gauge their effectiveness in managing emotions and fostering positive outcomes.

Reconciliation Plan:

1. Preparation: Mentally and emotionally prepare for reengagement by practicing self-compassion and forgiveness and letting go of resentment or negative emotions associated with past interactions.

2. Communication Strategy: Plan open and honest communication with individuals involved, expressing a desire for reconciliation and improved interactions going forward.

3. Proactive Listening: Prioritize listening to the perspectives and emotions of others without judgment, validating their experiences and feelings.

4. Empathy and Understanding: Demonstrate empathy and understanding towards the feelings and experiences of others, acknowledging any harm caused during past interactions.

5. Amends and Healing: Offer sincere apologies where necessary and take responsibility for any mistakes or hurtful actions you may have caused in the past, expressing a genuine commitment to repairing and strengthening relationships.

6. Collaborative Solutions: Collaborate with individuals to identify constructive solutions and strategies for better communication and conflict resolution in future interactions.

Expected Outcomes:

1. Emotional Healing: Initiate the healing process by addressing past interaction traumas and fostering forgiveness and understanding among all parties involved.

2. Relationship Repair: Rebuild trust and strengthen relationships through open dialogue, empathy, and mutual respect.

3. Improved Interactions: Encourage healthier and more positive interactions moving forward, characterized by effective communication, emotional awareness, and conflict resolution skills.

Conclusion:

By assessing the results of EQ improvement strategies and initiating the reconciliation process in past interactions, we aim to foster healing, repair relationships, and create a more harmonious and supportive environment for all parties involved.

ASSESSING YOUR IQ PROGRESS POST NEW STRATEGY

Transforming Your IQ: A Journey to Healing and Connection

Now that you've made that commitment to bolster your emotional intelligence (EQ) and have tracked your progress, you're ready to put into action your plan for better interactions with those of whom you've had a history of past interaction challenges often resulting in trauma.

During this process, try and pay closer attention to the reactions of others with whom you've decided to test out this new strategy and journal things such as their responses to your call for reconciliation and record cues such as hand gestures, facial expressions, and body language.

Doing this will give you insight into how others with which you'd had interaction challenges in the past receive your efforts to improve this relationship as we all know the old saying goes:

It takes two to "Tango!" As long as you make the best effort possible and show that you are a proactive participant and a willing partner in this effort, that's all you can ask for at this point.

Journal of Personal Growth and Interactions

Objective:

To implement and assess the effectiveness of a new strategy aimed at improving interactions with family, friends, colleagues, and individuals with whom I typically had difficult interactions, with the ultimate goal of fostering better outcomes and deeper connections.

Background:

In reflecting on past interactions, I recognized a pattern of trauma and tension stemming from unresolved conflicts and misunderstandings. These interactions often left me feeling drained, frustrated, and disconnected from those around me. Seeking growth and healing, I embarked on a journey to implement a new approach to communication and conflict resolution.

Methodology:

1. Mindfulness Practice: Prior to engaging in any interaction, I committed to centering myself through mindfulness techniques. This allowed me to approach conversations with a calm and grounded presence, reducing the likelihood of reactive responses.

2. Proactive Listening: I made a conscious effort to truly listen to the perspectives of others without judgment or interruption. This involved paraphrasing and summarizing their words to ensure mutual understanding.

3. Empathy Building: To cultivate empathy, I practiced putting myself in the shoes of the other person, seeking to understand their feelings, needs, and motivations. This facilitated greater compassion and connection.

4. Assertive Communication: Instead of suppressing my own thoughts and feelings, I learned to express them assertively and respectfully. This included using "I" statements and assertive body language to convey my perspective without imposing it on others.

5. Conflict Resolution Strategies: When conflicts arise, I will refrain from avoidance or aggression and instead approach them as opportunities for growth and understanding. I employed techniques such as proactive listening, validation of feelings, and collaborative problem-solving to reach mutually satisfactory resolutions.

Results:

1. Increased Emotional Resilience: By practicing mindfulness and self-awareness, I developed greater emotional resilience, allowing me to navigate challenging interactions with greater ease and composure.

2. Enhanced Empathy and Connection: Through active listening and empathy building, I forged deeper connections with others, fostering a sense of understanding and mutual respect.

3. Improved Conflict Resolution: By adopting assertive communication and conflict resolution strategies, I was able to address conflicts constructively, leading to more positive outcomes and strengthened relationships.

4. Reduced Stress and Anxiety: By approaching interactions with a proactive and compassionate mindset, I experienced reduced stress and anxiety associated with interpersonal conflicts.

Conclusion:

The implementation of this new strategy has been transformative, enabling me to break free from old patterns of interaction and cultivate healthier, more fulfilling relationships. Moving forward, I am committed to continuing this journey of personal growth and connection, knowing that each interaction presents an opportunity for deeper understanding and healing.

COMBINING THE TWO EFFORTS INTO ONE STRATEGY: LEVERAGING EQ & IQ FOR POSITIVE CHANGE

Now that we've got a good handle on where we stand with our new and improved EQ-IQ Relationship and have done the work by assessing each other and journaling our progress, it's time that we combine the two efforts to proactively effect change and begin the healing process with some individuals who represent our most challenging interactions.

We will begin with a leap of faith and boldly reach out to a friend or family member to begin the process of a new dialogue, changing years of poor communication leading to misunderstanding.

This might mean reaching out to your mother or father after so many years of silence. The thought of this could be traumatic in and of itself, but if you're going to tackle this head-on, then why not begin with sending a card or an email to open the possibility of a new dialogue.

Harnessing Emotional Intelligence for Transformative Interactions

Objective:

To integrate newfound insights into emotional intelligence (EQ) and past negative interactions, leveraging them to implement effective strategies for improved EQ during interactions with individuals with whom I've historically had challenges, even trauma.

Background:

Recognizing the impact of past negative interactions on my emotional well-being, I embarked on a journey of self-discovery and growth, delving into the realms of emotional intelligence and interpersonal dynamics. Armed with this knowledge, I now seek to apply it in real-world interactions to foster positive outcomes and heal past wounds.

Methodology:

1. Self-Awareness: Utilizing self-assessment tools and reflective practices, I have gained a deeper insight into my emotional triggers, patterns of behavior, and areas for growth. This heightened self-awareness serves as the foundation for improving my EQ during interactions.

2. Empathy Development: Drawing on my understanding of empathy and perspective-taking, I strive to empathize with the experiences and emotions of others, even those with whom I've had difficult interactions in the past. By acknowledging their perspectives and validating their feelings, I aim to build trust and connection.

3. Emotion Regulation: Employing mindfulness techniques and emotion regulation strategies, I endeavor to manage my own emotions effectively during interactions. By remaining calm and composed, I can respond thoughtfully rather than react impulsively, minimizing the risk of escalation or conflict.

4. Assertive Communication: Building on my assertive communication skills, I seek to express myself honestly and respectfully while also actively listening to the viewpoints of others. This balanced approach fosters open dialogue and promotes mutual understanding, even in challenging situations.

5. Conflict Resolution: Leveraging my newfound conflict resolution strategies, I approach conflicts as opportunities for growth and reconciliation. By engaging in constructive dialogue, seeking common ground, and exploring mutually beneficial solutions, I aim to resolve conflicts peacefully and restore harmony in relationships.

Results:

1. Empowered Interactions: By combining my understanding of emotional intelligence with insights from past interactions, I feel empowered to navigate challenging situations with confidence and grace.

2. Healing and Reconciliation: Through empathetic listening and assertive yet compassionate communication, I have initiated the process of healing past wounds and rebuilding trust with individuals who have been affected by negative interactions.

3. Strengthened Relationships: By prioritizing empathy, emotional regulation, and constructive conflict resolution, I have deepened

my connections with others and fostered healthier, more fulfilling relationships.

4. Personal Growth: This journey has not only enhanced my interpersonal skills but has also catalyzed profound personal growth, allowing me to transcend old patterns of behavior and embrace a more authentic and empowered way of relating to others.

Conclusion:

By integrating my newfound understanding of emotional intelligence with lessons learned from past interactions, I am poised to embark on a transformative journey of healing, growth, and positive change. Armed with empathy, self-awareness, and effective communication strategies, I am committed to fostering deeper connections and building a more harmonious and compassionate world, one interaction at a time.

YOUR NEW UNITED FRONT POST ASSESSMENT/ IMPLEMENTATION: EMBRACING EQ PROGRESS THROUGH THE JOURNEY TO HEALING & GROWTH

After deciding to reengage with at least one or two individuals with whom you've had a history of challenging interactions due to poor EQ habits, it's time to record results and ascertain whether your new strategies resulted in measurable progress and/or whether this needs to be tweaked.

Whether this resulting conflict was initiated by your unchecked EQ, with the person with which you've had the interactions or the atmosphere created by the two of you, it's time to celebrate small victories or reassess what other methodology to deploy for better outcomes.

At this point, journaling seems to be a more crucial task as it creates a detailed timeline of all events from the inception of the poor interactions leading up to the point where you've deployed these important strategies. A United Front is essential in reinforcing the support needed to grow.

Synopsis:

In this compelling narrative, follow the transformative journey of Jane, a resilient individual determined to navigate the complexities of emotional intelligence (EQ) to foster healthier interactions with those impacted by past communication traumas. Through heartfelt journal entries, Jane candidly shares the highs and lows of her quest for personal growth, celebrating even the smallest victories along the way.

Key Themes:

1. Emotional Intelligence: Delve into the exploration of self-awareness, self-regulation, empathy, and interpersonal skills as Jane embarks on her quest to enhance EQ.

2. Healing Past Traumas: Witness Jane's courageous efforts to confront and overcome the scars left by past negative interactions, using them as catalysts for growth rather than barriers.

3. Incremental Progress: Celebrate the significance of small victories and incremental steps forward, highlighting the importance of perseverance and resilience in the journey toward improved emotional intelligence.

4. 4. Supportive Allies: Experience the power of solidarity and the unwavering support of close allies and trusted confidants, who stand by Jane's side as she forges ahead on her path to self-discovery, growth, and healing from past traumas.

Impact and Takeaways:

Through Jane's introspective narrative, readers are invited to reflect on their own emotional intelligence (EQ) journey and find inspiration to embrace growth amidst adversity. This book promises to be a compelling exploration of resilience, healing, and the transformative power of emotional intelligence leading to a higher interaction quotient (IQ).

CHAPTER 5

"3-Ps" TO BETTER INTERACTIONS

THE "3-Ps" (PRACTICE, PRACTICE, PRACTICE)

I'm not here to remind you of the fact that with anything in life regarding achievable progress to a higher level, there's always that commitment component since this will sound more "preachy" than it would encouragement.

However, just as you would be going to your local gym on an almost daily basis, building muscle to stave off illness through your committing to stay on top of your health, you must use that same logic to approach and commit to your mental health and emotional intelligence as well.

Many people take their EQ for granted, just as some in society ignore their physical health to the extent that we have rampant issues of obesity, which in itself leads to major health concerns. So, it is your emotional intelligence that leads to undesirable results in our family interactions, in the workplace, and in everyday communication with others.

"3-Ps" TO BETTER INTERACTIONS

Introduction:

Meet Violet, a determined individual committed to enhancing her emotional intelligence (EQ) to cultivate more meaningful and harmonious interactions with those in her life. Recognizing the vital role EQ plays in fostering healthy relationships, Violet has devised a rigorous schedule of intentional practice aimed at achieving optimal results in her interpersonal interactions.

Setting the Stage:

Born out of a desire for personal growth and a genuine connection with others, Violet's journey towards mastering EQ begins with a deep introspection of her own emotional landscape. She acknowledges past challenges and recognizes the need for proactive measures to overcome them.

The Plan:

With unwavering dedication, Violet constructs a comprehensive schedule designed to immerse herself in various aspects of emotional intelligence. From daily mindfulness exercises to role-playing scenarios, each activity is meticulously curated to target specific areas for improvement.

Practice Makes Perfect:

Embracing the mantra of "practice, practice, practice," Violet commits wholeheartedly to her schedule, recognizing that true mastery of EQ requires consistent effort and dedication. She approaches each interaction as an opportunity for growth, applying newfound insights and strategies with intentionality, grace, and patience.

Challenges and Triumphs:

Along the way, Violet encounters obstacles and setbacks, confronting moments of frustration and self-doubt. Yet, fueled by her unwavering determination, she perseveres, drawing strength from each challenge as an opportunity for learning and growth. With each triumph, she celebrates the progress made, no matter how small, reaffirming her commitment to the journey.

The Road Ahead:

As Violet continues on her journey towards mastering emotional intelligence, she remains steadfast in her pursuit of deeper connections and more meaningful interactions. With each passing day, she embraces the transformative power of intentional practice, confident in her ability to foster positive change within herself and those around her.

Conclusion:

In Violet's quest for enhanced emotional intelligence, the path to success is paved with dedication, perseverance, and a steadfast commitment to intentional practice. Through her inspiring journey, she serves as a beacon of hope and inspiration, demonstrating that with determination and effort, anyone can cultivate the skills needed to thrive in both personal and professional relationships.

"3-Ps" TO BETTER INTERACTIONS

JOURNALING YOUR MORE RECENT INTERACTIONS

Incremental Growth: A Tale of Evolving Emotional Intelligence

Now that you see a timeline emerging from the time of the first entry in your journal of self-reflection and self-discovery to improve or EQ - IQ Ratio, as you see the emergence of incremental improvements in your interactions, you can now see your trajectory taking shape.

Congruent to this is the language or words you choose to describe your more recent interactions in that you could probably read an evolution in the entries emerge as well.

Your own self-awareness is another key factor in recognizing how far you've come as you read your earlier entries, comparing them to your more recent ones, as this improvement to the language in your writing is a byproduct of the effort to improve your overall EQ and interactions.

Introduction:

Step into the world of April, a courageous individual on a transformative journey towards enhancing her emotional intelligence (EQ) to foster deeper and more meaningful connections with those around her. Through introspective journal entries, April documents her gradual but remarkable progress, observing tangible growth in multiple aspects of her life.

Embracing Change:

As April reflects on her journey, she recognizes the subtle shifts taking place within herself. Where once there was uncertainty and hesitation, there now resides a newfound sense of confidence and clarity. Each entry serves as a testament to her evolving emotional landscape, marked by moments of insight and self-discovery.

Recognizing Growth:

In comparing her recent journal entries to those of the past, April is struck by the noticeable differences. Her newer entries brim with optimism and resilience, reflecting a deeper understanding of her emotions and a greater capacity for empathy and understanding. She celebrates the small victories, acknowledging the progress made with each passing day.

Integration into Daily Life:

Beyond the pages of her journal, April sees the impact of her journey manifesting in various aspects of her life. In her interactions with others, she approaches conversations with newfound compassion and authenticity, fostering stronger connections and healthier relationships. At work, she navigates challenges with a calm and composed demeanor, drawing upon her growing emotional intelligence to find effective solutions.

Navigating Challenges:

Though the growth path is not without its obstacles, April faces each challenge with resilience and determination. She embraces setbacks as opportunities for learning and growth, recognizing that true progress is often forged in the crucible of adversity. With each hurdle overcome, she emerges stronger and more resilient than ever before.

Looking Ahead:

As April continues on her journey of self-discovery, she remains committed to the pursuit of emotional intelligence. With each step forward, she embraces the unknown with courage and conviction, knowing that the path to personal growth is a lifelong journey. Through her inspiring example, she inspires others to embark on their own quest for self-improvement, one small step at a time.

Conclusion:

In the narrative of April's life, the journey of incremental growth is one marked by courage, resilience, and self-discovery. Through her introspective journal entries, she invites us to witness the transformative power of emotional intelligence, demonstrating that even the smallest steps forward can lead to a profound and lasting change.

ASSESSING RECENT INTERACTIONS WITHIN YOUR NEW COMFORT ZONE

Documenting EQ: A Chronicle of Incremental Growth

In addition to celebrating even the smallest of victories, you should also take time to perform quick assessments after each win-win interaction. Take your iPad or favorite Android Tablet/Device with you to meetings or to your local coffee house where you might take meetings.

I am one to be habitual as it relates to jotting down things or copious notes to the extent that I might ask the present company to allow me a few minutes should a thought or an inspiration arise. With that said, I believe the process is accelerated once you've recognized a positive change in the way your interactions are going with an individual or individuals with which you've had challenges in the past.

Walk away from those conversations with the thought that you feel a sea change in where you are with this individual, and you want to continue affecting change and solidify this new experience.

"3-Ps" TO BETTER INTERACTIONS

Synopsis:

In this captivating narrative, meet Jean, a determined individual committed to mastering the art of emotional intelligence (EQ) through meticulous documentation of her interactions with individuals from her past with whom communication has been challenging. Armed with a notebook and pen, Jean embarks on a journey of self-discovery, capturing every moment of incremental growth and transformation in real-time.

Key Themes:

1. On-the-Fly Documentation: Witness Jean's dedication to recording her journey of EQ growth in real-time, as she takes copious notes immediately after experiencing breakthroughs in communication with challenging individuals.

2. Incremental Growth: Explore the nuances of Jean's journey as she documents the subtle shifts and progressions in her interactions, celebrating each small victory as a milestone on the path to greater emotional intelligence.

3. Challenging Dialogue: Delve into the complexities of Jean's past interactions with challenging individuals as she navigates through moments of tension and conflict with grace and resilience.

4. Self-Reflection and Learning: Join Jean on her journey of self-discovery as she uses her documentation to reflect on her communication patterns, identify areas for improvement, and implement strategies for growth and positivity.

Impact and Takeaways:

Through Jean's meticulous documentation and unwavering commitment to self-improvement, readers are invited to reflect on their own communication habits and consider the transformative power of emotional intelligence.

This section promises a compelling exploration of resilience, self-reflection, and the journey toward meaningful connection through intentional communication to foster greater interactions.

STRIKING UP CONVERSATIONS WITH STRANGERS (W/SAFETY): A JOURNEY TO ENHANCE EQ THROUGH EVERYDAY INTERACTIONS

It is now time to test out your new EQ Strength with a few individuals with whom you have no history of interactions, so you go to the grocery store, and while in the produce section, you see an opportunity to make small talk about none other than the price of organic avocados.

You begin the conversation about making your favorite guacamole dip and then how you love to cook with the superfood, but you've noticed prices have "gone through the roof" of late.

While peeking into her cart, the conversation expands into a few other things you've observed she'd placed into her cart, so you talk about those items in comparison. Inadvertently, you are reminded that you need a few of those items you see in the cart, and you thank her for reminding you. Hence, your first interaction with a stranger feels (in a word…) liberating!

"3-Ps" TO BETTER INTERACTIONS

Synopsis:

In this inspiring tale of personal growth, follow the journey of Jean, a courageous individual ready to break free from her comfort zone and enhance her emotional intelligence (EQ) through meaningful interactions with strangers. From chance encounters at the grocery store to brief exchanges in line at a coffee shop or local retail stores like Target or Walmart, Jean embarks on a quest to foster genuine connections and enrich her social experiences.

Key Themes:

1. Courageous Exploration: Join Jean as she courageously steps out of her comfort zone, embracing opportunities for spontaneous dialogue with strangers in everyday settings.

2. Embracing Vulnerability: Witness Jean's willingness to embrace vulnerability as she opens herself up to the possibility of rejection and discomfort in pursuit of deeper connections.

3. Practice and Adaptability: Follow Jean as she hone her emotional intelligence skills through practice and adaptability, learning to navigate diverse social situations with grace and authenticity.

4. Celebrating Small Victories: Experience the joy and fulfillment Jean finds in celebrating even the smallest victories—a genuine smile, a shared laugh, or a brief moment of connection—as she gradually builds confidence and rapport with strangers.

Impact and Takeaways:

Through Jean's journey of self-discovery and interpersonal growth, readers are encouraged to embrace the power of stepping outside their comfort zones and engaging with others with authenticity. This section promises to display a heartwarming exploration of courage, vulnerability, and the transformative potential of everyday interactions in fostering emotional intelligence and enriching the lives of all involved.

JOURNALING YOUR CONVERSATIONS WITH STRANGERS: A JOURNAL OF SELF-DISCOVERY & EMOTIONAL GROWTH

After engaging with a few strangers in your travels a time or two, you now have enough information to tabulate your results and plot a course for these impromptu conversations so you take out your favorite iPad or Android Tablet or perhaps you're the old fashion type and you carry around a notebook to journal.

In either case, you're now ready to record each interaction with strangers and note how you felt about the outcomes. You begin to reflect on how the conversation flowed and the ease at which you were/are engaging while using mere small talk to initiate.

In a separate entry, you do a quick comparison to earlier conversations and underscore your progress with each interaction. You notice your confidence has grown since you started and you're now becoming more and more comfortable at each incremental step of the process.

Synopsis:

Dive into the fascinating world of Lora, an individual committed to harnessing the power of emotional intelligence (EQ) through meaningful interactions with strangers. Armed with courage and curiosity, Lora embarks on a journey of self-discovery, documenting each conversation in a journal as she navigates the nuances of small talk in pursuit of a genuine connection.

Key Themes:

1. Embracing Vulnerability: Join Lora as she bravely steps outside her comfort zone to engage strangers in conversation, embracing vulnerability as a pathway to deeper connection and personal growth.

2. The Art of Small Talk: Explore the intricacies of small talk as Lora navigates through everyday interactions, honing her skills in active listening, empathy, and authenticity.

3. Measuring Progress: Follow Lora's journey of self-reflection and growth as she meticulously journals each conversation, noting observations, insights, and areas for improvement to measure her progress over time.

4. Acknowledging Imperfection: Witness Lora as she acknowledges that growth is a journey, not a destination, and celebrates both the triumphs and the setbacks along the way, recognizing that every interaction is an opportunity for learning and growth.

Impact and Takeaways:

Through Lora's candid exploration of human connection and emotional intelligence, readers are invited to reflect on their own interactions with strangers and consider the transformative power of vulnerability and authenticity. This section promises a thought-provoking journey of self-discovery, resilience, and the pursuit of genuine connection in the increasingly disconnected world we live in today.

CHAPTER 6

AVOIDING TRIGGERS

REVISITING UNCOMFORTABLE CONVERSATIONS

Courage in Conversation: A Journey of Reflection and Healing

After you have begun the process of reaching out to an estranged old friend or family member whose relationship you once held dear, don't expect this initial contact to be received with overwhelming joy or a sense of gratitude for initiating the contact.

These attempts to reengage with others estranged could often be met with doubt, skepticism, pessimism, or even a tinge of paranoia in one case, questioning whether I've reached out to ask a favor or something of the sort.

Not to worry, because once you get through the first layer of that wall that's been there since the separation, you can now begin the process of reestablishing trust and rekindling the joy you once experienced with that old friend or loved one.

Introduction:

Step into the world of Kate, a resilient individual embarking on a courageous journey of reconciliation and healing. After years of silence and separation, Kate finds the strength to revisit uncomfortable conversations with others despite the initial challenges and resistance encountered along the way.

Confronting Discomfort:

For Kate, the decision to revisit uncomfortable conversations was not made lightly. Years of silence weighed heavily on her heart, and she knew that in order to move forward, she must confront the discomfort head-on. Despite the fear of rejection, she resolved to take the first step towards healing old wounds.

Facing Resistance:

Initially, Kate's attempts to reconnect were met with skepticism and reluctance from those she reached out to. Old wounds resurfaced, and the scars of past misunderstandings seemed too deep to overcome. Yet, Kate remained undeterred, understanding that healing old wounds would not be an easy process but deeming it necessary for her own growth and peace of mind.

Accepting the Journey:

With each rejection and setback, Kate found solace in the knowledge that healing is not linear. She accepted that the journey toward reconciliation would be filled with ups and downs, but she remained steadfast in her commitment to reaching out and fostering understanding with those from her past.

Journaling the Experience:

Throughout her journey, Kate diligently journaled her experiences, capturing the raw emotions and insights that emerged from each conversation. These journal entries served as a source of reflection and guidance, allowing Kate to navigate the complexities of reconciliation with grace, hope, and resilience.

Embracing Hope:

As Kate continues on her journey of reconciliation, she embraces the courage to face uncomfortable conversations with hope and resilience. Though the road may be rocky, she remains committed to healing old wounds and forging deeper connections with those she cares about, one conversation at a time.

Conclusion:

In Kate's story, we find inspiration in the transformative power of courage and resilience in the face of discomfort. Through her unwavering commitment to healing old wounds and fostering understanding, Kate reminds us that reconciliation is possible, even after years of silence, separation, and past trauma.

JOURNALING UNCOMFORTABLE CONVERSATIONS

Reconnecting Through Reflection: A Journey to Healing

They say that forgiveness is more for the person doing the forgiving than for the recipient and so it is with the revisiting of interactions trauma with those with whom you've had a history of uncomfortable conversation; so approach this new effort to engage with humility, vulnerability and a chance at reconciliation.

AVOIDING TRIGGERS

During this new journey of self-discovery, it is inevitable that we will be confronted with those uncomfortable conversations, which led to the years of separation should we decide to reengage with individuals with which we've had challenging interactions in the past.

We must look at this as an opportunity to heal old wounds and change the trajectory of this history of interaction trauma. It helps if you've kept a journal from which to compare once these issues surface, but it's not necessary since we have a new chance to journal from here.

Introduction:

Enter the world of Jane, a courageous individual on a journey of self-discovery and reconciliation. After years of silence and separation resulting from uncomfortable conversations and triggers, Jane is determined to rewrite the narrative and forge a new path toward meaningful connection with those from her past.

Facing Triggers:

For too long, Jane allowed unresolved triggers and discomfort to dictate her interactions, leading to years of silence and separation from individuals who once held significance in her life. Each uncomfortable conversation became a barrier, further widening the gap between herself and those she cared about.

A New Chapter Begins:

With a renewed sense of purpose and determination, Jane embarks on a journey to reengage with these individuals and rewrite the narrative of their relationships. Armed with introspection and a commitment to growth, she approaches each interaction with an open heart and a willingness to confront past wounds.

Comparing Experiences:

In her quest for reconciliation, Jane finds solace and guidance in revisiting old journals, where she documented the pain and discomfort of past interactions. By comparing these experiences with her new journal entries, Jane gains invaluable insights into her own transformation, recognizing the progress made and the distance traveled since those tumultuous times.

Reflecting on Growth:

As Jane navigates through uncomfortable conversations with newfound courage and resilience, she reflects on how she has evolved and matured. No longer bound by the silence of the past, she embraces vulnerability as a catalyst for healing and transformation, forging deeper connections and fostering understanding with those she once feared to confront.

Changing the Trajectory:

Through Jane's inspiring journey, readers are reminded of the transformative power of self-reflection, forgiveness, and the courage to confront discomfort head-on. This narrative serves as a testament to the resilience of the human spirit and the boundless potential for growth and healing, even in the face of the past pain and separation of interactions trauma.

REPLAYING SCENARIOS FOR A BETTER OUTCOME

Rehearsing Resilience: Preparing for Difficult Conversations with Trusted Allies

Not that you've revisited some of your past uncomfortable interactions, which in some cases led to years of separation, and journaled your experiences where you were able to reconnect and notated those who didn't respond, you're now ready to compare notes and reenact these interactions with that trusted friend or confidant with which you began this process.

For the sake of clarity, your purpose for replay with this trusted friend is to parse out those most difficult exchanges, which led to the misunderstanding ultimately leading to separation.

You are armed with your powerful journal, which holds the key to your interactions quotient history, both past and present, so you now go through line by line with your confidant, replying to the once toxic-speak with a more enlightened EQ and the benefit of retrospect.

Synopsis:

In this empowering narrative, witness the journey of Suzzie, a courageous individual determined to confront past toxicity and reclaim her voice in challenging conversations. Seeking to bolster her confidence and resilience, Suzzie enlists the support of trusted friends and confidants to rehearse and prepare for difficult interactions with individuals from her past.

Key Themes:

1. Facing Past Toxicity: Join Suzzie as she bravely revisits some of her most difficult and uncomfortable conversations, confronting past toxicity with courage and determination.

2. Seeking Support: Explore the transformative power of seeking support from trusted allies and confidants as Suzzie enlists their help in rehearsing and preparing for challenging interactions.

3. Building Confidence: Follow Suzzie as she hones her communication skills and bolsters her confidence through role-playing and constructive feedback, empowering herself to navigate difficult conversations with grace and resilience.

4. Reclaiming Her Voice: Witness Suzzie as she takes ownership of her narrative and refuses to be silenced by past experiences, reclaiming her voice and asserting her boundaries with conviction and authenticity.

Impact and Takeaways:

Through Suzzie's courageous journey of self-discovery and empowerment, readers are reminded of the importance of seeking support and preparation when confronting challenging conversations. This one-sheet promises a thought-provoking exploration of resilience, empowerment, and the transformative potential of reclaiming one's voice in the face of adversity.

In a courageous act of self-reflection and preparation, Suzzie decides to revisit some of her most difficult and uncomfortable conversations with a trusted friend or confidant. Recognizing the importance of bolstering her confidence before reengaging with the individuals who have been the source of toxic interactions, Suzzie seeks the support of someone she trusts implicitly. Together, they carefully replay the scenarios, dissecting each exchange with honesty and compassion and exploring potential strategies for navigating similar situations in the future.

Suzzie sought solace and support from a trusted friend or confidant as she revisited some of her most difficult and uncomfortable conversations. Recognizing the importance of bolstering her confidence before reengaging with the individual who had been the source of toxic interactions, Suzzie leaned on her confidant for guidance and perspective.

Together, they meticulously replayed the conversations, dissecting each exchange with care and compassion. With her friend by her side, Suzzie found the strength to confront her fears head-on and to anticipate potential challenges with grace and resilience. Through this process, she not only gained valuable insights and strategies for navigating future interactions but also felt empowered to reclaim her voice and assert her boundaries with confidence and conviction.

With her trusted friend by her side, Suzzie finds solace in the opportunity to practice assertiveness and boundary-setting, knowing that she is not alone in her journey toward healing and growth.

Through this process, Suzzie gains valuable insights into her own communication patterns and triggers, empowering her to approach future interactions with a newfound sense of confidence and resilience. Armed with the support of her confidant and a renewed sense of self-assurance, Suzzie feels better equipped to face whatever challenges may arise during her next revisit, knowing that she has taken proactive steps to prepare herself for whatever may come her way.

ASSESSING YOUR TRIGGERS

Empowering Growth: Proactively Learning from Past Triggers

In this journey of self-reflection, there is that aspect where certain triggers stand out as a reminder of a time when there were words spoken that completely up-ended the conversation.

Of course, the new you go into these conversations with not only a keen awareness of what these triggers are but also an action plan to avoid allowing them to devolve into the interaction abyss.

Whether alone or with your trusted friend, you assess your EQ before, during, and after these triggers caused your conversation to take its turn for the worse so you are now prepared to handle a similar situation with more grace, empathy, and humility.

Introduction:

Meet Becky, a resilient individual on a proactive journey of self-discovery and growth. Having experienced toxic interactions with family and friends due to past triggers, Becky is determined to delve deep into her mindset, guard against vulnerabilities, and cultivate grace and empathy in her interactions. With the support of a trusted friend and confidant, she prepares herself for future interactions with those who have caused her pain.

Acknowledging Past Triggers:

For Becky, the first step towards healing is acknowledging the past triggers that have led to toxic interactions. Reflecting on these experiences with honesty and vulnerability, she identifies the patterns and behaviors that have contributed to the breakdown of relationships with loved ones.

Guarding Against Vulnerabilities:

Armed with self-awareness, Becky takes proactive measures to guard against vulnerabilities to these triggers. Through introspection and mindfulness practices, she cultivates a deeper understanding of her emotions and reactions, empowering herself to respond with grace and empathy in challenging situations.

Practicing Grace and Empathy:

With the guidance of her trusted friend and confidant, Becky engages in role-playing exercises to practice responding to triggering situations with grace and empathy. By simulating difficult interactions and receiving constructive feedback, she hones her communication skills and prepares herself for future encounters with family and friends.

Embracing Growth and Resilience:

As Becky progresses on her journey, she embraces the growth and resilience that comes from confronting past triggers with courage and compassion. Rather than allowing herself to be defined by past experiences, she chooses to learn from them, empowering herself to foster healthier and more meaningful connections with those around her.

Conclusion:

In Becky's inspiring narrative, we find a testament to the transformative power of self-awareness, empathy, and proactive growth. Through her commitment to learning from past triggers and practicing grace and empathy, she serves as a beacon of hope and inspiration for others on their own journeys of healing and self-discovery.

AVOIDING TRIGGERS

With a steadfast commitment to personal growth and healing, Becky embarks on a proactive journey of self-discovery and mindfulness. Recognizing the detrimental impact of past triggers on her interactions with family and friends, she courageously confronts these challenges head-on, determined to learn from past experiences and cultivate a mindset of grace and empathy.

Enlisting the support of a trusted friend and confidant, Becky engages in reflective conversations and practices, delving deep into her mindset to identify and guard against vulnerabilities to these triggers. Through this intentional process, she prepares herself for future interactions with those individuals who have caused her pain, equipping herself with the resilience and compassion needed to navigate potential triggers with grace and empathy.

As Becky embraces this journey of self-awareness and growth, she recognizes that true healing and transformation require a proactive approach. By proactively addressing past triggers and vulnerabilities, she empowers herself to respond to challenging interactions with intentionality and compassion rather than allowing them to dictate her reactions.

With each practice session and conversation with her trusted friend, Becky strengthens her emotional resilience and fortifies her ability to maintain boundaries while extending grace to others. Through this process of self-discovery and preparation, Becky lays the foundation for healthier, more fulfilling relationships built on mutual understanding and empathy.

RINSE & REPEAT FOR BETTER OUTCOMES

Mastering EQ: A Cycle of Practice, Reflection, and Growth

What does this section: Rinse and repeat mean? It means what it says. It's time that you set goals to execute your strategy in cycles. This means you begin with Journaling your week and make notes of interactions at work, with family, and in everyday interactions at the grocery store, or on the line getting coffee.

I would recommend color-coding with highlighters next to these interactions from the past week, with GREEN being the *most positive* and RED being the *most challenging*; YELLOW means *needs work,* and LIGHT BLUE means *opportunity for growth* somewhere in between.

Perhaps you love PINK. Then, by all means, use PINK as your go-to instead of GREEN, using that for something else next to your journal entry.

Synopsis:

In this captivating narrative, follow the transformative journey of Florence, a resilient individual committed to mastering the art of emotional intelligence (EQ) for more rewarding interactions with those from her past with whom she's experienced toxic relationships. Through a cycle of effective practice and journaling, Florence embarks on a quest for EQ mastery, leveraging each experience as an opportunity for growth and self-discovery.

Key Themes:

1. Effective Practice: Join Florence as she engages in deliberate and intentional practice to enhance her communication skills and

emotional intelligence. From role-playing exercises to real-life interactions, each practice session is carefully designed to target specific areas for improvement.

2. Reflective Journaling: Explore the power of reflection and self-discovery as Florence diligently journals her experiences and insights. Through introspective writing, she gains valuable perspective on her communication patterns, emotional triggers, and areas for growth, paving the way for continuous improvement.

3. Breaking the Cycle: Witness Florence as she breaks free from the cycle of toxic relationships by cultivating a deeper understanding of herself and her interactions with others. With each practice session and journal entry, she takes proactive steps toward building healthier and more rewarding connections.

4. Achieving Mastery: Follow Florence on her journey towards EQ mastery as she embraces the iterative process of practice, reflection, and growth. With unwavering determination and resilience, she strives to achieve a higher level of emotional intelligence, transforming her relationships and her life in the process.

Impact and Takeaways:

Through Florence's inspiring journey, readers are invited to embark on their own quest for emotional intelligence mastery. This one-sheet promises a thought-provoking exploration of resilience, self-discovery, and the transformative power of deliberate practice in fostering healthier and more rewarding interactions.

In her relentless pursuit of EQ mastery and meaningful communication, Florence finds herself entrenched in a "rinse and repeat" cycle of effective practice and journaling. Each interaction becomes an opportunity for growth as she applies newfound insights and strategies gleaned from her reflective journal entries. With unwavering dedication, she meticulously analyzes past encounters, identifying areas for improvement and refining her approach for future interactions. Through this iterative process of practice and reflection, Florence steadily enhances her communication skills, inching closer to achieving EQ mastery and fostering more rewarding interactions with those she has encountered toxic relationships in the past.

CHAPTER 7

CELEBRATE BETTER RESULTS!

READING & CELEBRATING YOUR JOURNAL PROGRESS

Celebrating Growth: A Journey of Reflective Journaling to EQ Mastery

Whether you have a history of journaling that goes back several years or even decades, or you've just gotten into the habit of journaling as a result of this newfound journey you've recently undertaken, I'm sure at this point you have an idea of the power of this journaling tool.

Journaling has the power to transform many, if not all aspects of your life if leveraged in everyday practice as it is intended in this book. It is now time that you read and celebrate the progress journaling has revealed over the weeks and months that you deployed this awesome tool.

I like doing a comparison from the first entry to its more recent relevant entry to get an idea of how my journal writing has evolved over time. Pay particular attention to the language you used from the time of your earlier entries until today, and celebrate the result of your EQ progression.

Synopsis:

Embark on an inspiring journey of personal growth and emotional intelligence (EQ) mastery with Nina, a dedicated journaler whose reflective writings have become a testament to her transformative evolution over the past decade. From humble beginnings to exponential growth, Nina celebrates the profound impact of journaling on her journey toward greater self-awareness, empathy, authenticity, and a higher interaction quotient (IQ).

Key Themes:

1. Decade of Reflection: Join Nina as she revisits her journal entries spanning over a decade, marveling at the profound transformation captured within the pages. Through introspection and self-discovery, she traces her journey from uncertainty to confidence, from turmoil to tranquility.

2. Exponential Growth: Witness the remarkable progression in Nina's emotional intelligence as reflected in her journal entries. With each passing year, she experiences a tangible upward trajectory in her ability to navigate complex emotions, cultivate empathy, and foster healthier interactions, translating into better relationships with those around her.

3. Language of Celebration: Delve into the vibrant language of celebration as Nina joyously recounts her milestones and victories in her journal. Gone are the days of self-doubt and hesitation; Nina now embraces each entry with a sense of pride and accomplishment, celebrating her growth and resilience in the face of adversity.

4. Inspiring Others: Through her compelling narrative, Nina inspires readers to embark on their own journey of self-discovery and journaling, recognizing the transformative power of reflection and intentionality in fostering personal growth and emotional well-being.

Impact and Takeaways:

Through Nina's uplifting story, readers are reminded of the profound impact of reflective journaling in cultivating emotional intelligence and celebrating personal growth. This section promises a heartwarming exploration of resilience, self-discovery, and the limitless potential for positive change through the power of reflection and celebration.

In the sacred space of her journal, Nina has cultivated a sanctuary of growth and self-discovery over the past decade. What began as mere scribbles of thought and emotions has evolved into a testament to her exponential growth, particularly in the realm of emotional intelligence (EQ). With each entry, she unveils a mosaic of introspection, empathy, and wisdom, reflecting a journey marked by profound transformation and upward progression.

Now, as she celebrates the remarkable strides she has made in her EQ journey, Nina infuses her journal with a language of celebration and triumph. Her words dance with gratitude and joy, radiating the glow of newfound self-awareness and resilience. Through the language of her journal, Nina honors the journey that has brought her to this moment of profound growth and invites others to join her in celebrating the power of self-discovery and personal evolution.

ASSESSING YOUR EQ-IQ IMPROVEMENTS

A Progress Report on Enhancing EQ for Better Interactions

Just as it is with assessing each aspect of this journey, it is also important that you do the same with respect to your EQ to IQ Progression, and your Journal Entries hold the key to this as well.

Where you might have given yourself lower grades of your earlier EQ to IQ in retrospect, you are now equipped with enough information to see actual progress and tangible results, so be honest with yourself as it can only accelerate your efforts from this moment on.

Synopsis:

Join Sally on her transformative journey towards enhancing emotional intelligence (EQ) for more fulfilling interactions with family, friends, and colleagues. Several months ago, Sally embarked on this journey with a determination to cultivate greater self-awareness, manage her emotions effectively, and navigate interpersonal dynamics with grace and empathy. As she reflects on her progress, Sally notices a significant improvement in the way she responds to certain triggers, demonstrating a remarkable shift in her emotional intelligence (EQ) to interactions quotient (IQ).

Key Themes:

1. Self-Awareness: Sally's journey begins with a deep dive into self-awareness, as she recognizes the patterns and triggers that have hindered her interactions in the past. Through introspective journaling and reflection, she gains clarity on her emotional responses and areas for growth.

2. Emotion Regulation: Armed with newfound self-awareness, Sally learns to regulate her emotions more effectively, allowing her to respond thoughtfully rather than react impulsively in challenging situations. She no longer falls prey to old triggers, demonstrating a heightened ability to maintain composure and perspective.

3. Empathy and Understanding: Sally's journey towards EQ mastery extends beyond self-awareness and emotion regulation to encompass empathy and understanding towards others. She learns to see situations from different perspectives, fostering deeper connections and resolving conflicts with empathy and compassion.

4. Measuring Progress: Sally measures her progress by comparing her current responses to triggers with those documented in her earlier journal entries. Through this self-assessment, she witnesses tangible evidence of her growth and transformation, celebrating the milestones achieved along the way.

Impact and Takeaways:

Through Sally's journey, readers are invited to reflect on their own emotional intelligence and interpersonal interactions. Sally's progress serves as a beacon of hope and inspiration, demonstrating that with dedication and self-awareness, anyone can cultivate the skills needed to foster healthier and more rewarding relationships in all aspects of life.

This section promises a compelling exploration of resilience, growth, and the transformative power of emotional intelligence in interpersonal interactions.

CELEBRATING YOURSELF FOR EACH WIN!

Celebrating Victories: A Journey to EQ Mastery and Giving Back

I don't know about you, but I've learned over time to celebrate myself and every win, both great and small, as this attitude of gratitude is in alignment with striving to be your best self.

If you're asking me how I celebrate small victories, I would say in very different ways, whether it be treating myself to my favorite meal at an exclusive restaurant or donating to my favorite charity and paying it forward. Of course, you don't have to wait to donate, but in my humble opinion, there's a special memory in linking the donation to the act of celebration in your journal.

Synopsis:

Experience the heartwarming tale of Emily, a determined individual on a journey of self-discovery and emotional intelligence (EQ) mastery. Eager to celebrate her small victories and progress in fostering more rewarding interactions with loved ones and colleagues, Emily treats her confidant to a luxurious dining experience at their favorite 5-star sushi restaurant. In addition, she extends her celebration of growth by donating $100 to the local children's hospital, where she volunteers her time whenever she's not traveling for work in journals about the entire experience.

Key Themes:

1. Small Victories: Join Emily as she celebrates the incremental progress she has made on her EQ journey. From managing her

emotions effectively to fostering deeper connections with others, Emily recognizes and celebrates each small victory along the way.

2. Rewarding Interactions: Through intentional practice and reflection, Emily has cultivated more rewarding interactions with family, friends, and colleagues. By prioritizing empathy, understanding, and effective communication, she has fostered stronger bonds and resolved conflicts with grace and compassion.

3. Giving Back: In addition to celebrating her own growth, Emily extends her generosity to those in need by donating to the local children's hospital. Her dedication to volunteering reflects her commitment to making a positive impact in her community and spreading joy and compassion wherever she goes.

4. Gratitude and Reflection: As Emily savors her meal at the sushi restaurant and reflects on her journey, she is filled with gratitude for the progress she has made and the support of her confidant. She finds fulfillment in giving back to others and recognizes the importance of gratitude and generosity in her ongoing EQ journey.

Impact and Takeaways:

Through Emily's inspiring story, readers are reminded of the power of celebration, gratitude, and giving back in fostering personal growth and emotional well-being. Emily's journey serves as a testament to the transformative power of EQ mastery and the ripple effect of kindness and generosity in creating a more compassionate and connected world. This section promises a heartwarming exploration of resilience, growth, and the joy of celebrating life's small victories.

GIVING YOURSELF MORE TIME TO IMPROVE

Navigating Setbacks with Grace: A Journey of EQ Enhancement

As the old cliché goes: Rome wasn't built in a day. So, it is with the journey you are on to improve your interaction quotient (IQ). Thinking of it as a "journey" allows you to give yourself the grace you need and the time it takes to heal old mental and psychological wounds you experienced before you began your mission of self-discovery and EQ-IQ transformation.

Synopsis:

Step into the transformative journey of Joana, a resilient individual committed to enhancing her emotional intelligence (EQ) for more rewarding interactions and fulfilling relationships with family, friends, and colleagues. Along the way, Joana encounters setbacks and hiccups but learns the invaluable lesson of giving herself grace and time as she addresses years, even decades, of interactions and trauma stemming from unchecked EQ.

Key Themes:

1. Resilience in Adversity: Join Joana as she navigates through setbacks and hiccups on her EQ journey with unwavering resilience and determination. Despite facing challenges, she refuses to be discouraged, recognizing that growth takes time and perseverance.

2. Self-Compassion and Grace: Witness Joana as she learns the art of giving herself grace and compassion during moments of difficulty. Instead of harsh self-criticism, she embraces self-

compassion, understanding that healing from past trauma is a process that requires patience and understanding.

3. Acknowledging Trauma: Through introspection and reflection, Joana acknowledges the years of interactions and trauma stemming from unchecked EQ. She confronts past wounds with courage and vulnerability, recognizing the importance of addressing underlying issues to pave the way for genuine growth and healing.

4. Embracing the Journey: Despite the challenges, Joana remains committed to her journey of enhancing emotional intelligence. With each setback, she gains valuable insights and learns important lessons, strengthening her resilience and deepening her understanding of herself and others.

Impact and Takeaways:

Through Joana's inspiring journey, readers are reminded of the importance of resilience, self-compassion, and patience in the pursuit of emotional intelligence and fulfilling relationships. Her story serves as a beacon of hope and inspiration for anyone navigating their own journey of growth and healing, demonstrating that with grace and perseverance, transformation is possible. This one-sheet promises a poignant exploration of resilience, self-discovery, and the transformative power of self-compassion in the face of adversity.

JOURNALING MILESTONES

Turning the Page: Celebrating Milestones & Breakthroughs in Jessy's Journey

It is now time to turn the page in your journal and begin a new chapter called **Milestones**.

What should you record in this section, you might ask? To begin with, you are recording moments of significance, such as the events that led to reconnecting with an old friend, the new beginning with that estranged loved one, or the reconciliation of an ex for the sake of your children.

Synopsis:

Join Jessy as she turns the page to a new chapter in her journal, marking a significant milestone in her journey of growth and self-discovery. In this section titled "Milestones," Jessy celebrates breakthroughs of profound significance, including the reconnection with an old friend, the reconciliation with an estranged family member, and the long-awaited healing and reconciliation with her ex-partner, with whom she shares a relationship with their children following a contentious divorce as they now enjoy better interactions (IQ).

Key Themes:

1. Reconnection with Old Friend: Experience the joy and nostalgia as Jessy reconnects with a dear old friend, reigniting a bond that transcends time and distance. Their reunion serves as a reminder of the enduring power of friendship and the importance of nurturing meaningful connections.

2. Reconciliation with Estranged Family Member: Witness the emotional journey as Jessy embarks on the path towards reconciliation with an estranged family member. Through courage, forgiveness, and open-hearted communication, they bridge the divide and rebuild their relationship on a foundation of love and understanding.

3. Healing and Reconciliation with Ex-Partner: Journey alongside Jessy as she navigates the complexities of healing and reconciliation with her ex-partner, with whom she shares a history of conflict and contention. Through patience, empathy, and a shared commitment to co-parenting their children, they mend past wounds and forge a new, harmonious relationship built on mutual respect and cooperation.

Impact and Takeaways:

Through Jessy's milestones and breakthroughs, readers are invited to reflect on the transformative power of forgiveness, reconciliation, and the resilience of the human spirit. This section promises a poignant exploration of healing, growth, and the profound significance of meaningful connections in her journey toward fulfillment and authenticity.

CHAPTER 8

SECURING YOUR DREAM JOB!

MASTERING EMOTIONAL INTELLIGENCE: A JOURNEY TO PROFESSIONAL SUCCESS

So, you've reached a milestone in terms of your EQ to IQ Progress, and now you're ready to test it out in professional circles, so you decide to find a job posting that is close to your dream job. Whether it be writing for the local or national newspaper or periodical or advancing your current career aiming for a more lofty goal, you're excited to research and prepare for this opportunity.

Sarah's Story

Sarah, a dedicated professional, embarked on a transformative journey to enhance her Emotional Intelligence (EQ) to improve interactions across various spheres of her life. Through diligent self-reflection, empathy exercises, and communication workshops, Sarah honed her ability to navigate relationships with friends, family, and colleagues with empathy, understanding, and assertiveness.

Armed with newfound confidence derived from her enhanced EQ, Sarah sought to put her skills to the test in the realm of professional development. Having experienced more rewarding interactions, including successful job interviews, she decided to take a bold step forward. Sarah identified her dream job posting, recognizing it as an opportunity to showcase her improved emotional intelligence in a high-stakes scenario.

Key Achievements:

1. Enhanced Interpersonal Skills: Sarah mastered the art of active listening, effective communication, and conflict resolution, fostering deeper connections with individuals in her personal and professional life.

2. Increased Self-awareness: Through introspection and mindfulness practices, Sarah gained a deeper understanding of her own emotions, motivations, and triggers, enabling her to respond thoughtfully rather than react impulsively in various situations.

3. Empathy and Understanding: Sarah cultivated empathy as a cornerstone of her interactions, demonstrating a genuine interest in others' perspectives and feelings, which fostered trust and collaboration.

4. Confidence in Job Interviews: Sarah's improved EQ translated into successful job interviews, where she showcased her authentic self, communicated her strengths effectively and connected with interviewers on a deeper level.

Future Endeavors:

Eager to continue her growth journey, Sarah aims to leverage her refined emotional intelligence not only in her dream job but also as a mentor and advocate for others seeking personal and professional development. She envisions a future where empathetic leadership and authentic connections are valued and embraced across all aspects of society.

Conclusion:

Sarah's story exemplifies the transformative power of emotional intelligence in fostering fulfilling relationships and professional success. Her journey serves as an inspiration for individuals seeking to cultivate meaningful connections and navigate life's challenges with grace and authenticity.

DOING YOUR RESEARCH/REACHING OUT TO YOUR NETWORK

Sally: Empathetic Trailblazer Pursuing her Dream Job

Now that you've gained the confidence, which comes as a direct result of this EQ Journey leading to better Interactions in all aspects of your life, you are ready to test out your growth in your professional career and aspirations.

Ok, I must admit this exercise might be a bit challenging, although not impossible, in the pursuit of securing your dream job, but I wouldn't shy away from pursuit thereof because it may be difficult as the company could only say "no" or "not at this time."

To be totally transparent, this worked for me a few times when I was an IT Consultant as I'd always wanted to work for Multinational Entertainment Companies, so this is based upon experience and not just putting pen to paper, so to speak.

Sally's story

A determined individual with a passion for personal growth is embarking on a transformative journey to become a more emotionally intelligent (EQ) being. Armed with newfound skills acquired through introspection, learning, and practice, she aims to revolutionize her approach to interactions and relationships.

Driven by the desire to secure her dream job, Sally recognizes the invaluable role emotional intelligence plays in professional success. Understanding that effective communication, empathy, and self-awareness are essential in today's competitive landscape, she is committed to honing these skills to perfection.

Sally's dedication extends beyond mere ambition; she actively engages in research, devouring insights into industry trends, company culture, and the expectations of her potential employers. By meticulously preparing for potential interviews, she ensures she can confidently demonstrate her enhanced emotional intelligence and its relevance to the role she aspires to.

In Sally's pursuit of her dream job, her journey towards greater emotional intelligence isn't just a personal endeavor—it's a strategic advantage. By leveraging her newfound skills, she not only aims to excel professionally but also to inspire positive change in her workplace and beyond. Sally is not just seeking a job; she's on a mission to become an empathetic trailblazer, transforming her interactions and making a lasting impact and impression wherever she goes.

That's fantastic! Sally's proactive approach will surely pay off. Researching for a potential interview is a crucial step in the preparation process. Here are some key areas Sally might want to focus on:

1. Company Research: Understanding the company's history, mission, values, and recent news can demonstrate genuine interest and enthusiasm during the interview. It also helps Sally tailor her responses to align with the company culture.

2. Job Description Analysis: By thoroughly analyzing the job description, Sally can identify the key skills and experiences the company is looking for. She can then prepare examples from her own experiences that highlight these skills.

3. Self-Reflection: Sally should take some time to reflect on her own experiences, skills, strengths, and weaknesses. Being able to articulate these effectively during the interview can help her stand out as a candidate.

4. Practice Behavioral Interview Questions: Many interviews include behavioral questions that require candidates to provide specific examples of past experiences. Sally can practice answering these types of questions using the STAR method (Situation, Task, Action, Result) to structure her responses effectively.

5. Networking: If possible, Sally could reach out to current or former employees of the company to gain insights into the

company culture and interview process. Networking can also help her get her foot in the door and potentially secure a referral.

6. Technical Skills Review: Depending on the nature of the job, Sally may need to brush up on specific technical skills or knowledge relevant to the position. This might involve reviewing industry trends, tools, or software.

7. Mock Interviews: Conducting mock interviews with a friend, family member, or mentor can help Sally practice articulating her thoughts and responses in a professional setting. It also provides an opportunity to receive constructive feedback.

By investing time and effort into thorough preparation, Sally can enter her interview feeling confident, well-informed, and ready to showcase her skills and qualifications.

SETTING UP THE INTERVIEW FOR YOUR DREAM JOB

Selina's Journey to Pursue Her Dream Job

Now that you've done your due diligence and have reached out to some in your network for that insider information about the position(s) available, you are ready to reach out to the HR Department for that position for which you're the best fit.

Let's say that you're happy with your current full-time employment and you have more lofty goals of honing your skills to write that book, paint that landscape, or record that track since it's been some time since you've picked up a microphone.

I'm a believer in cultivating your "entire self," and your EQ journey to better interactions speaks to the need to attend to your best Creative Self as well.

Summary:

Selina, a seasoned professional with years of diverse industry experience, is embarking on an inspiring journey to pursue her dream job in a field completely new to her. Driven by a passion for a talent she cultivated since childhood but set aside during her career pursuits, she is ready to step out of her comfort zone and seize this opportunity.

Background:

Selina boasts a rich history of success in various industries, accumulating a wealth of skills and expertise along the way. Despite her accomplishments, she has always harbored a deep-seated desire to immerse herself in a specific field—one that aligns perfectly with her lifelong passion.

Motivation:

Fueled by a relentless determination to fulfill her aspirations, Selina is ready to break free from the confines of familiarity and embrace the challenge of pursuing her dream job head-on. Her decision is fueled not only by professional ambition but also by a longing to reignite the flame of her childhood talent, which has lain dormant for much too long.

Transformation:

Embracing the unknown, Selina is prepared to leverage her transferable skills and adaptability to navigate the nuances of an unfamiliar industry. Her journey represents a testament to resilience, courage, and the unwavering pursuit of one's true calling.

Goals:

Selina's primary objective is to secure a position within a company that embodies the essence of her dream job, allowing her to apply her diverse skill set while immersing herself in a field she is truly passionate about. Additionally, she aims to reignite her dormant talent, nurturing it back to its former glory and incorporating it into her professional endeavors.

Conclusion:

Selina's journey is a testament to the transformative power of chasing one's dreams, even in the face of uncertainty and unfamiliarity. With her unwavering determination, vast experience, and renewed passion, she is poised to embark on a remarkable chapter in her professional and personal growth, embracing the unknown with open arms and a heart full of ambition.

APPLYING YOU'RE NEW IQ & MEASURING SUCCESS

SoJourner's Quest for Her Dream Job

Great news! You've landed that interview, and you over-prepare for this first of three rounds. Your first round of interviews will be with HR, which will be a 20-30-minute initial interview to see if you're a good fit for a dynamic company culture.

Your second round will consist more of subject-matter and behavioral questions, and your third (should you progress that far…) will be to meet the team and sit down with your future boss and/or team lead. Piece of cake…right?

Summary:

SoJourner, a driven and ambitious young woman, has embarked on a quest to secure her dream job in a field that resonates deeply with her passions and aspirations. Armed with a newfound mastery of emotional intelligence (EQ), she eagerly anticipates the opportunity to showcase her skills and forge meaningful connections throughout the interview process.

Background:

SoJourner's journey is marked by her unwavering determination to pursue her career aspirations with vigor and enthusiasm. Drawing upon her rich network of connections, she has diligently sought out opportunities aligned with her professional goals, ultimately leading her to the threshold of her dream job.

Motivation:

Driven by a relentless pursuit of personal and professional growth, SoJourner views each step of the interview process as a chance to demonstrate her aptitude, showcase her passion, and connect authentically with her prospective employers. Her excitement is palpable as she embraces the opportunity to put her EQ mastery to the test, fostering genuine interactions and leaving a lasting impression.

Transformation:

SoJourner's journey represents a transformative odyssey fueled by her unwavering ambition and commitment to self-improvement. Through her dedicated pursuit of emotional intelligence, she has honed her ability to navigate interpersonal dynamics with grace and finesse, positioning herself as a compelling candidate poised for success.

Goals:

SoJourner's primary goal is to navigate the interview process with confidence, poise, and authenticity, leveraging her EQ mastery to establish rapport, convey her qualifications, and articulate her vision for the role. With each round of interviews, she aims to deepen her connections, showcase her unique strengths, and leave a lasting impression on her prospective employers.

Conclusion:

As SoJourner embarks on this pivotal chapter of her professional journey, she approaches each round of interviews with a sense of optimism, enthusiasm, and determination. With her newfound EQ mastery as her guiding light, she is poised to navigate the complexities of the interview process with grace and finesse, ultimately realizing her dream of securing that elusive dream job or gaining more confidence for stepping out of her comfort zone in the first place.

JOURNALING MILESTONES OF THIS NEWFOUND EXPERIENCE: EMBRACING THE JOURNEY

After you've gone through this liberating experience of getting out of your comfort zone and flexing this newfound confidence of yours as a result of your journey to EQ Mastery, you are now ready to journal the entire experience from beginning to end. In these more recent journal entries lies the secret to your successes of late and the lynchpin to your continual growth within this personal journey to EQ Mastery for greater, more rewarding interactions.

Synopsis:

Tracey is a determined and resilient individual who fearlessly stepped out of her comfort zone to pursue her dream job. Throughout the interview process, she garnered praise and accolades for her exceptional skills and potential contributions. However, despite her stellar performance, Tracey faced the disappointment of learning that the company opted for an internal candidate deeply entrenched within the organization's culture and ecosystem.

Key Points:

1. Courageous Pursuit: Tracey's decision to pursue her dream job showcases her courage and determination to challenge herself and pursue her passions.

2. Positive Reception: Throughout the interview process, Tracey received glowing reviews, indicating her competency and suitability for the role.

3. Unexpected Outcome: Despite her impressive performance, the company ultimately decided to select an internal candidate, emphasizing the importance of existing cultural fit and integration within the organization.

4. Resilience and Optimism: Despite the setback, Tracey maintains a positive outlook and records the experience as a personal victory in her journal. She sees it as a stepping stone towards her future endeavors.

5. Future Opportunities: The company has assured Tracey that she will be seriously considered for future positions, demonstrating recognition of her potential and leaving the door open for future collaboration.

Conclusion:

Tracey's journey highlights the importance of resilience, courage, and optimism in the face of adversity. While her initial setback may seem disappointing, it serves as a valuable learning experience and a testament to her unwavering determination to pursue her dreams. As she continues on her path, Tracey remains poised to seize future opportunities and make a meaningful impact in the field of her dream job and aspirations.

CHAPTER 9

ATTITUDE OF GRATITUDE CONCEPTS

DEPLOYING GRATITUDE & EMPATHY IN YOUR INTERACTIONS

From Interpersonal Turmoil to Emotional Intelligence Mastery

So you've practiced with your confidant and put in many hundreds of hours on this journey to strive for deeper, more meaningful interactions, and you do see a noticeable difference. As been stated before, this new you has translated in all important areas of your life and you now feel you have a good handle on how to respond in everyday situational interactions. This posture has given you a new and renewed purpose to deploy concepts of gratitude.

Synopsis:

In just a few short months, Suyen has undergone a remarkable transformation in her quest to enhance her emotional intelligence

ATTITUDE OF GRATITUDE CONCEPTS

(EQ) and elevate her interactions with others. Formerly plagued by tumultuous encounters with family, friends, and colleagues, many of which left scars of interactional trauma, Suyen has emerged from the shadows with a newfound sense of purpose and direction.

Key Points:

1. The Journey: Suyen's path to emotional intelligence mastery has been anything but easy. She faced numerous challenges and setbacks in her interactions, often leaving her feeling overwhelmed and defeated. However, instead of succumbing to despair, she chose to confront her shortcomings head-on, determined to break free from the cycle of negativity.

2. The Transformation: Through dedication and perseverance, Suyen has made significant strides in improving her EQ. She has learned to recognize and manage her emotions more effectively, allowing her to respond to situations with clarity and composure rather than reacting impulsively. This newfound emotional resilience has enabled her to navigate difficult conversations and conflicts with grace and poise.

3. Embracing Gratitude: One of the most profound shifts in Suyen's journey has been her adoption of an attitude of gratitude. Rather than dwelling on past grievances or focusing on what she lacks, she now approaches each interaction with a sense of appreciation and abundance. This shift in her perspective has not only enriched her own life but has also deepened her connections with others, fostering more meaningful and fulfilling relationships.

4. The Future: As Suyen continues to hone her emotional intelligence skills, she looks forward to a future filled with even deeper

and more authentic interactions. Armed with newfound self-awareness and empathy, she is confident in her ability to navigate life's challenges with grace and resilience, forging connections that are built on trust, understanding, and mutual respect.

Suyen's journey serves as a testament to the transformative power of emotional intelligence and the profound impact it can have on both personal and professional relationships. Her story is a reminder that no matter where we are in our journey, it is never too late to cultivate greater self-awareness, empathy, and gratitude, paving the way for a brighter and more fulfilling future.

YOUR INTERACTIONS HAVE BEEN OFF THE CHARTS!

Embracing Gratitude: Suyen's Transformational Journey

With this new posture, you've noticed a consistency in the way you've engaged in meaningful conversations, and now others are beginning to notice as well, so you continue to journal their reactions along with your own. Some might think you're not being authentic, and you want to have them believe this is the new you. This speaks more about them and not you, as it may take some time for some to believe you've undergone a transformation in the way you interact.

Synopsis:

Suyen's journey towards a new attitude of gratitude has sparked a wave of introspection and change among her family members and friends, especially those who have experienced challenges in their interactions with her in the past. While acknowledging that this transformation is a marathon rather than a sprint, Suyen remains committed to building upon her successes. She finds solace in the moments when her newfound approach is embraced, recognizing that it will take time for others to fully embrace the change.

Details:

Suyen's shift towards gratitude has been met with a mixture of surprise, relief, and admiration from those closest to her. Many have noticed a significant change in her demeanor and interactions, which has positively impacted their relationships. Friends and family members who have previously faced challenges in their interactions with Suyen now find her more empathetic, vulnerable, understanding, and willing to listen.

One of the key aspects of Suyen's journey is her acknowledgment that change doesn't happen overnight. She understands the importance of patience and perseverance, recognizing that building genuine connections based on gratitude requires time and effort. Despite occasional setbacks, Suyen remains steadfast in her commitment to growth and self-improvement.

The reception of Suyen's transformation varies among her social circle. Some have embraced her new attitude wholeheartedly, expressing gratitude for the positive change they've witnessed. Others remain skeptical or hesitant, unsure of whether Suyen's transformation is genuine or fleeting. Nevertheless, Suyen remains undeterred, cherishing each moment of progress and remaining open to feedback and reflection from these doubtful sources.

As Suyen continues on her journey of gratitude, she serves as an inspiration to those around her. Her perseverance and dedication remind others of the power of self-reflection and personal growth. Through her example, Suyen demonstrates that change is possible, even in the face of past challenges and resistance.

In conclusion, Suyen's newfound attitude of gratitude is reshaping her relationships and leaving a lasting impact on those around her. While the journey may be long and challenging, Suyen remains committed to growth and transformation, cherishing each step forward and embracing the support of her trusted friends and loved ones along the way.

CULTIVATING SOFT SKILLS IN YOUR COMMUNICATIONS

"Empowering EQ: A Journey of Personal Growth Toward Leadership"

So you've now gotten the attention of your leadership at work as others have lauded you and your efforts to become a more valued team member as a result of this journey you've been on for several months now. For their part, the company leadership is considering either hiring a team lead from a pool of candidates on the outside through referrals or from the current org chart.

As a result of what the team has told management about you of late, you have now been vaulted to the top of their list for this coveted leadership role; now you've added "soft skills" to the list.

Synopsis:

In the bustling professional landscape, one individual's commitment to enhancing Emotional Intelligence (EQ) stands out as a testament to the power of self-awareness and growth. Meet Joyce, a dedicated team member who embarked on a transformative journey to refine her EQ, igniting a ripple effect of positive change in her interactions in the workplace.

Overview:

Joyce's journey toward enhancing her EQ began with a realization of its pivotal role in effective communication and collaboration. Recognizing the importance of understanding emotions, both her own and those of her colleagues, she delved into various resources, workshops, and self-reflection exercises.

As Joyce diligently honed her EQ skills, her colleagues began to take notice of her remarkable growth. They praised her newfound ability to navigate challenging situations with empathy, defuse conflicts gracefully, and foster a more inclusive and harmonious work environment. Her genuine connections and empathetic approach not only improved team dynamics but also boosted morale and productivity.

Turning Point:

The culmination of Joyce's journey occurred when her leadership team took notice of her remarkable transformation. Impressed by her demonstrated EQ prowess and its positive impact on team dynamics, they began considering her for a team lead role—a testament to her invaluable contributions and potential for leadership.

Next Steps:

Buoyed by the recognition of her peers and the interest in her leadership, Joyce now sets her sights on further refining her soft skills in anticipation of this new role. Eager to embrace the responsibilities and challenges of leadership, she embarks on a proactive quest to enhance her communication, conflict resolution, and decision-making abilities.

Conclusion:

Joyce's journey from EQ seeker to potential team lead exemplifies the transformative power of personal growth and self-awareness in the professional realm. Her commitment to fostering meaningful connections, nurturing a supportive work culture, and continuously refining her soft skills serves as an inspiration to her colleagues and a beacon of hope for aspiring leaders everywhere. As she continues to evolve and empower others, Joyce embodies the essence of effective leadership rooted in emotional intelligence and genuine human connection.

GIVING YOURSELF A LITTLE GRACE... & TIME

Support To Leadership Journey

You are now front and center in your most challenging role to date, and you're facing some on the team who would rather be more combative than embrace you as the new team lead so you seek the advice of the former team lead with whom you understood to be an effective leader.

In this conversation, you've learned quite a bit about the strengths and weaknesses of the team overall and have now formulated strategies to move the team forward in this very demanding environment. Just give yourself a little grace and time for your new strategies to take effect.

A little background on Mina, who has been an integral part of the company's support team for several years, demonstrating unwavering dedication and a strong work ethic. Throughout her tenure, she has consistently displayed a passion for helping others and a knack for problem-solving, making her a valued member of the team for the foreseeable future.

Promotion to Leadership:

Recognizing her potential and commitment, company leadership made the bold decision to promote Mina to a leadership role. This decision was rooted in her journey to bolster her soft skills, which caught the attention of upper management. Her newfound leadership position is a testament to her growth and development within the company.

Challenges:

Transitioning from a supportive role to a leadership position hasn't been without its challenges. Despite the recognition from higher-ups, not all members of the team have readily accepted Mina as their new leader. However, rather than being discouraged, she has chosen to approach this obstacle with grace and patience, understanding that gaining trust and respect takes time.

Approach:

In her quest to become an effective leader, Mina is taking proactive steps to ease into her new role. She understands the importance of listening and learning from those who have come before her. By sitting down with the former team lead to listen attentively and take notes, she demonstrates humility and a genuine desire to understand the dynamics of her team.

Future Outlook:

While the journey to fully embrace her leadership role may be a gradual one, Mina is committed to putting in the effort and dedication needed to succeed. With her positive attitude, willingness to learn, and determination to grow, she is poised to make a meaningful impact as a leader within the company.

JOURNALING MILESTONES

Now that you've begun your new journey as team lead with the arduous task of leading some that you've served on the same level with for years, the difficult task of acceptance is underway. After you've sat down with the former team lead to listen and learn the nuances of the team, you're now journaling this milestone on day one of your new leadership role.

Transitioning Support Professional to Team Lead

Summary:

Sarah Miller, a dedicated support professional with several years of experience in the company, has recently stepped into a new leadership role. Her journey from a support role to leadership is marked by her commitment to enhancing her soft skills, which garnered the attention of the management, leading to her promotion. Despite the acknowledgment from higher-ups, Sarah faces the challenge of acceptance from some members of her team who may not readily embrace her in this new role.

ATTITUDE OF GRATITUDE CONCEPTS

Background:

Having served diligently in various support capacities over the years, Sarah's dedication and drive did not go unnoticed by the leadership. Recognizing her potential, they decided to elevate her to a leadership position where she could leverage her soft skills with a heightened EQ to lead and inspire her team. However, the transition is not without its hurdles, particularly with team members who may have reservations about her new role.

Approach:

Sarah approaches her new role with a blend of humility and determination. Understanding that transitioning into leadership requires time and patience, she chooses to give herself grace and space to grow into the position. One of her key strategies is to actively seek guidance and feedback from her predecessor, acknowledging the wealth of knowledge and experience they possess.

Action Plan:

On day one of her new role, Sarah initiates a journaling practice to document her journey and reflect on her experiences daily. This allows her to track her progress, identify areas for improvement, and celebrate milestones along the way. Additionally, she implements strategies such as regular team meetings to foster open communication, team-building activities to strengthen bonds, and mentorship programs to support individual growth within the team.

Outcome:

Through her commitment to personal growth and her proactive approach to leadership, Sarah aims to earn the trust and respect of her team members over time. By embracing challenges as opportunities for learning and development, she sets herself on a path toward becoming a confident and effective leader who leads by example and empowers her team to achieve success together as a unit.

CHAPTER 10

EQ - IQ MASTERY

YOU'VE ARRIVED HERE

Take a deep breath now that you've arrived here. Where is "here," you might ask? Well, here is where you have discovered you're no longer the person in the room who is afraid, nor are you unsure of yourself in situations where certain language used in conversations will trigger you.

You've arrived at a destination on an emotional trajectory that you've worked hard to achieve and one in which you took control, assessing long ago that it was "you" holding you back and not others in your orbit or the society at large. You decided to do the work to improve your EQ!

EMPATHETIC RESILIENCE: JOURNEY TO EQ MASTERY

Synopsis:

In a world where emotional triggers often dictate reactions, Fiona stands as a beacon of empathetic resilience. Having embarked on a transformative journey towards Emotional Intelligence (EQ) mastery, she has arrived at a serene destination where external triggers hold no power over her.

Character Description:

Fiona is a resilient individual who has navigated through the labyrinth of her emotions, emerging victorious with newfound clarity and confidence. Her journey to EQ mastery has been marked by introspection, self-discovery, and unwavering determination.

Through dedicated practice and introspective reflection, Fiona has cultivated a deep understanding of her own emotions and triggers. Armed with this self-awareness, she has developed the invaluable skill of emotional regulation, allowing her to remain composed and centered in the face of adversity.

Fiona approaches conversations with an open mind and a compassionate heart. While she acknowledges the presence of triggers, she no longer allows them to dictate her reactions or cloud her judgment. Instead, she embraces each interaction as an opportunity for growth and understanding, navigating through potentially challenging conversations with grace and empathy.

With a newfound sense of inner peace and confidence, Fiona stands tall, ready to embrace the path forward with optimism and resilience. Her journey to EQ mastery serves as an inspiration to others, reminding them of the transformative power of self-awareness, empathy, and emotional resilience in a quest for a higher, more rewarding Interactions Quotient.

LEVERAGING YOUR NEW IQ

As covered a previous chapters, you should view each interaction as an opportunity to learn and share more without divulging (TMI) too much information about yourself unless the conversation warrants that you go deeper than you would normally; after all, this is not a psycho-therapy session.

However, going into these conversation opportunities, you have the benefit of a track record that proves your preparation readies you for any surprises; therefore, you can trust the process.

Embracing Connection: Harnessing EQ As An Impetus for IQ Mastery

Synopsis:

In a world where past traumas often dictate present interactions, Juliet stands as a testament to the transformative power of Emotional Intelligence (EQ). Through dedication and self-reflection, she has harnessed the strength of her EQ to navigate difficult interactions and forge meaningful connections with those she once found challenging.

Character Description:

Juliet is a resilient individual who has embarked on a journey of self-discovery and growth, leveraging the principles of EQ to overcome past traumas and embrace the full spectrum of human connection. Her story is one of courage, vulnerability, and unwavering determination.

Having experienced difficult interactions and trauma in the past, Juliet once found herself shying away from individuals with whom she shared a tumultuous history. However, armed with newfound EQ skills, she has found the courage to confront these past demons and engage with these individuals with empathy, honesty, and compassion.

Through intentional practice and introspection, Juliet has developed a deeper understanding of her own emotions and triggers, allowing her to navigate through potentially challenging interactions with grace and poise. She no longer allows past traumas to dictate her present interactions but instead approaches each encounter with an open heart and a willingness to listen attentively and understand.

By embracing her EQ growth, Juliet has unlocked a newfound sense of confidence and comfort in interacting with others across all facets of life. Whether it be in professional settings or personal relationships, she approaches each interaction as an opportunity for growth and connection, fostering deeper bonds and enriching her life in profound ways.

Juliet's journey serves as a beacon of hope for those who have experienced similar struggles, reminding them that with resilience, self-awareness, and empathy, it is possible to transcend past traumas and embrace the beauty of human connection.

EVERYDAY LIFE CAN BE REWARDING

We in society often hear the old cliché "Life is what you make it!" Well, with a little bit of hard work and ingenuity, life can be very rewarding when you move past, allowing interactions and trauma from your past to dictate your day-to-day life. So, let's begin to change the narrative today!

Embracing EQ: Crafting a Fulfilling Narrative through Everyday Interactions

Synopsis:

In a world inundated with fast-paced schedules and fleeting connections, Jill emerges as a beacon of intentional living and meaningful engagement. Having embarked on a transformative journey to enhance her Emotional Intelligence (EQ), she now champions the belief that everyday life holds immense potential for gratifying interactions and personal growth. Armed with a newfound mantra—"Everyday Life Can Be Most Rewarding in how one interacts on a daily basis"—Jill navigates life's intricacies with purpose, empathy, and authenticity.

Key Points:

1. Transformation Through EQ Development: Jill recognized the need for a shift in her approach to interpersonal dynamics. Through dedicated efforts and self-reflection, she embarked on a journey to cultivate her Emotional Intelligence. By honing skills such as self-awareness, empathy, and effective communication, she has unlocked a deeper understanding of herself and others.

2. Embracing Intentionality: No longer content with surface-level interactions, Jill embraces the power of intentionality in her daily encounters. Whether it's a conversation with a colleague, a spontaneous encounter with a stranger, or a heartfelt exchange with a loved one, she infuses each interaction with mindfulness and authenticity.

3. Finding Fulfillment in the Ordinary: Jill rejects the notion that fulfillment is reserved for grand milestones or extraordinary

experiences. Instead, she finds joy and satisfaction in the simple moments of connection that pepper her daily life. Whether it's sharing a laugh with a friend, offering a listening ear to a coworker, or expressing gratitude to a family member, she recognizes the profound impact of these seemingly mundane interactions.

4. Championing a New Narrative: With her enhanced EQ and newfound perspective, Jill serves as a catalyst for positive change in her community. By leading by example and spreading her mantra of rewarding daily interactions, she inspires others to cultivate deeper connections, foster empathy, and embrace the richness of everyday life.

Letter To Yourself:

In a world characterized by hustle and bustle, Jill stands as a testament to the transformative power of Emotional Intelligence (EQ) for more rewarding interactions (IQ). Through her commitment to intentional living and meaningful interactions, she proves that everyday life is indeed most rewarding when approached with empathy, authenticity, and purpose.

ENTERING INTO INTERACTIONS BLISS!

I know what you're thinking. You're thinking is "interactions bliss" really a thing? Yes, interactions bliss is really a thing, but it doesn't come easy without staying present in the moment and responding with intentionality in your conversations.

This doesn't mean these conversations will always go the way we'd hope, but you can at least walk away knowing in your heart of hearts that you responded in such a way that you were true to yourself and the conversation without feeling a sense of guilt or betrayal to your new mantra.

The Quest for Interactions Bliss: Journey Towards EQ Mastery

Synopsis:

Meet Abby, an individual on an extraordinary quest for Interactions Bliss through the mastery of Emotional Intelligence (EQ). Having dedicated thousands of hours over the years to personal development, Abby stands poised at the pinnacle of her journey, ready to infuse every interaction with profound resonance for both herself and those with which she's fortunate enough to engage in meaningful conversations.

Details:

1. Abby has embarked on a relentless pursuit of understanding and honing Emotional Intelligence, recognizing its pivotal role in fostering meaningful connections.

2. Through meticulous self-reflection, empathetic listening, and continuous learning, Abby has cultivated a profound awareness of her own emotions and those of others, laying the foundation for authentic and transformative interactions.

3. Every encounter is viewed by Abby as a precious opportunity to contribute positively to the lives of others, enriching both parties involved.

4. With each interaction, Abby imparts a signature inspirational quote, encapsulating the essence of the exchange and leaving a lasting impression on those she encounters.

5. Gratitude permeates Abby's interactions, as she expresses sincere thanks for the time and attention of others, recognizing the value of each moment shared.

Vision:

Abby's journey exemplifies the power of Emotional Intelligence in fostering meaningful connections and nurturing a culture of empathy and understanding. Through her quest for Interactions Bliss, she inspires others to embark on their own path toward EQ mastery, creating a ripple effect of positivity and connection in the world.

JOURNEY TO INTERACTIONS BLISS: MASTERING EQ & AMPLIFYING ENCOUNTERS

Synopsis:

Meet Karen, an individual on a relentless quest to achieve Interactions Bliss through the mastery of Emotional Intelligence (EQ). After investing thousands of hours in self-reflection, study, and practice, she stands poised to transform every interaction into a reverberating symphony of connection and mutual understanding.

Background:

Having dedicated years to understanding the intricacies of human emotions and social dynamics, Karen has cultivated a profound awareness of herself and others. Through diligent journaling, she meticulously documents each encounter, extracting valuable insights and honing her ability to navigate the complex nuances of human interaction.

Quest for Interactions Bliss:

Driven by an insatiable thirst for connection and growth, Karen approaches every interaction as an opportunity for mutual elevation. Armed with her arsenal of EQ skills, she navigates conversations with empathy, authenticity, and intentionality, leaving a lasting impact on everyone she encounters.

The Journal of Interactions:

Within the pages of her journal, Karen immortalizes the essence of each interaction, capturing the subtle nuances, emotions, and revealings that unfold in the moment. From fleeting encounters to profound conversations, every detail is meticulously documented, serving as a roadmap on her journey towards Interactions Bliss.

Amplifying the Ripple Effect:

As Karen continues to refine her EQ mastery, the ripple effect of her interactions extends far beyond herself. Each exchange becomes an opportunity to create positive change, fostering deeper connections, fostering understanding, and inspiring others to embark on their own quests for Interactions Bliss.

Conclusion:

With unwavering dedication and boundless compassion, Karen exemplifies the transformative power of Emotional Intelligence (EQ) in fostering meaningful connections and elevating every interaction to a state of blissful resonance. As she continues to journey forward, her impact on the world around her only grows stronger, one heartfelt connection at a time.

©2024 NeuEarth Media.
All Rights Reserved.

Made in the USA
Columbia, SC
07 October 2024